Special Praise for

T0032245

"*Pothead* captures a giddy, buzzy, unprecedented moment
in our culture—a new, outwardly joyful wave of reefer
madness that takes its toll. Neal has always been a hilarious
writer, but also surprisingly reflective and bravely self
insightful. His latest book is as funny as always,
but also bracingly, movingly sober."

John Hodgman, comedian and author
of *Vacationland* and *Medallion Status*

• • •

"You don't have to be a pothead to appreciate the
humor and pathos in *Pothead*, Neal Pollack's zippy,
deep-thinking Gen-X recovery memoir."

Caroline Kepnes, author of *You*

• • •

"In the recovery movement, they might call the first half of
Neal Pollack's *Pothead* a war story, for its impressively rich
catalogue of indignities and pratfalls. But as in all the best
war stories, Pollack's account is rendered with such spirit
and wit, with such a bottomless arsenal of hilarities that it is
impossible to look away. We long throughout this harrowing
account for the moment when Neal Pollack's feet will strike
the earth, and when he does, his considerable talent billows
out with a bright new reflective aspect. This is an especially
lucid and welcome account, therefore, of a long journey
through compulsion into clarity, insight, and acceptance."

Rick Moody, award-winning author
of *The Black Veil* and *The Ice Storm*

• • •

"Neal Pollack's *Pothead* is a harrowing corrective to the popular myth that marijuana use is always safe and consequence-free. Told with ruthless honesty and Pollack's signature irreverence, it delineates how a seemingly harmless habit can devolve into a life-ruining addiction, and what it takes to come back. This is a valuable, timely addition to our cultural conversation about marijuana, and a gift to anyone who loves fearless memoir laced with dark wit."

Kristi Coulter, author of *Nothing Good Can Come from This*

• • •

"Neal Pollack's memoir tells a story of an addiction very different from mine. His drugs of choice were marijuana and gambling. But, as is so very often the case with stories of recovery, his story is very much the same as mine. Addiction is addiction, after all.

"Pollack's writing is heartbreaking, funny, tender, and honest. And it offers great hope for the growing numbers who are finding themselves addicted to marijuana in this legal age of weed. I read this book in one sitting. It's that good and it's that helpful. All at the same time."

Dana Bowman, author of *Bottled* and *How to Be Perfect Like Me*

POTHEAD

NEAL POLLACK

POTHEAD

MY LIFE AS A
MARIJUANA ADDICT
IN THE AGE
OF LEGAL WEED

CENTRAL RECOVERY PRESS

LAS VEGAS

Central Recovery Press (CRP) is committed to publishing exceptional materials addressing addiction treatment, recovery, and behavioral healthcare topics.

For more information, visit www.centralrecoverypress.com.

Publisher: Central Recovery Press
             3321 N. Buffalo Drive
             Las Vegas, NV 89129

25 24 23 22 21 20   1 2 3 4 5

Library of Congress Cataloging-in-Publication Data
Names: Pollack, Neal, 1970- author.
Title: Pothead : my life as a marijuana addict in the age of legal weed /
    Neal Pollack.
Description: Las Vegas : Central Recovery Press, 2020. | Summary: "Renowned
    author Neil Pollack chronicles his journey from marijuana addiction to
    marijuana recovery in this eye-opening memoir"-- Provided by publisher.
Identifiers: LCCN 2019054973 (print) | LCCN 2019054974 (ebook) | ISBN
    9781949481303 (paperback) | ISBN 9781949481310 (ebook)
Subjects: LCSH: Pollack, Neal, 1970- | Drug addicts--United
    States--Biography. | Marijuana abuse--United States. | Marijuana
    abuse--Rehabilitation--United States. | Authors, American--21st
    century--Biography.
Classification: LCC HV5822.M3 P65 2020 (print) | LCC HV5822.M3 (ebook) |
    DDC 362.29/5092 [B]--dc23
LC record available at https://lccn.loc.gov/2019054973
LC ebook record available at https://lccn.loc.gov/2019054974

Photo of Neal Pollack by Regina Allen.

Cover design by The Book Designers.

Interior by Sara Streifel, Think Creative Design.

CONTENTS

PART ONE: STONED

Free America	3
What a Dope	11
A Member of the Rock Star Poet Literary Elite	17
A Cool Stoner Dad	27
The Long Night of My Trivia Soul	35
The Weird Turn Pro	63
Ganja Yoga	69
The Baklava of Death	81
Post-Trebek Stress Disorder	89
Mother Died Today	99
The Hand You're Dealt	121
No More Death	133
There's No Crying in Baseball	139

PART TWO: SOBER

163	Out of the Fog
169	Powerless
173	The Problem with Poker
185	Sober Tent
189	The Dream Dog Appears
199	Daddy Issues
207	The Heart of the Matter
223	No Weddings and a Funeral
232	Acknowledgments

PART ONE:

STONED

FREE AMERICA

The sun had already gone down by the time Rich and I crossed the golden border from New Mexico to Colorado. We looked at each other, free at last. For the first time in our lives, we could legally smoke marijuana in our home country. And all it had taken, in the Year of Our Lord 2014, was driving a minivan through a mountain pass.

"I don't have any weed on me," said Rich, a burly and cuddly middle-aged stoner dad who, like me, worked from home. "But if I did, it would be okay."

I opened the window and breathed the sweet mid-December mountain air. At the time, Pueblo was the first place across the border where you could buy pot. We still had a hundred miles to drive. We followed our TomTom directions, getting increasingly excited as we headed toward a new and glorious future.

We had arrived in Free America.

I was embarrassed that it had taken me that long to get to Colorado. Of all the writers I know—really, of all the humans I know—I was the biggest, most fervent, most frequent stoner. So it was beyond pathetic that it took me a year to get to the Holy Land, especially because I had the free time.

All summer, I sat around getting high in Texas and saying, "I really should head up to Colorado for a couple of weeks." I could have done it at pretty much any point; instead, I just sat back and watched as unqualified CNN reporters got their tours of airplane hangars full of marijuana plants, as Dr. Sanjay Gupta, of all people, became medical marijuana's biggest advocate. For Bob Marley's sake, even Maureen Dowd went to Denver and got high.

I was missing the revolution. But even the last person who arrives at the party gets to attend.

To get to legal pot before closing time, we'd left Austin at 8:30 a.m., and that only worked because we gained an hour on the way. We drove the entirety of the Texas Panhandle, skirting Lubbock and Abilene and passing through downtown Amarillo, followed by nearly two hours of barren New Mexico high desert. It took forever and was unimaginably boring. Rich summed up the absurdity: "You can go down the street and buy an automatic weapon whenever you want. But you have to drive twelve hours to get legal weed."

Pueblo was Free America's stoner port of call, hosting the first dispensaries across the border. It sat five hours from Amarillo, about ten hours from Dallas, and a flat 800 miles from my home in Austin. Later, the town of Trinidad, Colorado, a mere thirteen miles from the New Mexico border, began to sell pot. That changed everything, shaving ninety minutes off the journey, thereby flooding Trinidad with eager, glassy-eyed Dallas bros. But at the time, Pueblo was the crossing.

I figured the pot store would be on a street or in a strip mall. Instead, it was at least fifteen minutes off the interstate.

We drove through a dark, industrial area punctuated by brushy vacant lots. There were no other cars around. I was to learn that Pueblo didn't allow marijuana sales within the city limits yet, meaning that all pot had to be sold on the county outskirts. At the time, though, it felt like we were going to buy pot like we always had: in the skeeziest possible circumstance.

But the similarities to the old ways ended there. At around 7:30 p.m., we pulled into a well-lit parking lot in front of a modest, but neat, brown stucco building. At the entrance to the parking lot was a little stone structure with a sign that read, simply, "Cannasseur." We walked inside, into a high-ceilinged room that looked like an ordinary waiting area, except that there were enormous high-definition photographs of marijuana buds hanging everywhere. The pilgrims had arrived at the temple.

A smiling young woman sat behind the desk.

"Welcome to Cannasseur," she said. "Can I see your IDs?"

We handed them over.

"We've had lots of people from Texas today," she said.

The budtender was busy with another customer. It would just be a couple of minutes. We paced around the room like nervous dogs at the vet. Then the woman stood up, opened the door to the inner chamber, and said, "Enjoy."

The angels sang as we entered paradise. Along the black-painted walls sat dozens of jars of marijuana, of the highest possible quality and of every possible type, as well as candy bars, sodas, balms, tinctures, oil cartridges, and sour gummies, in seemingly infinite varieties. There were joints under glass. The room smelled sweet and danky. It was amazing.

I'd had a medical card in California for years, so I more or less knew what to expect. But I still walked around in there grinning, happier than Hank Hill at Home Depot. All artifice had been removed from the process.

Rich had never been to a dispensary before. His expression was even more gee-whiz. We were in an alternate drugstore from another dimension. This was legal!

The budtender, a chill guy wearing a straight-brimmed baseball cap, looked up. He held small shears in his right hand.

"Just doing my trimming," he said, like it was the most natural thing in the world.

"That's cool," I said.

"You're in luck," he said. "It's happy hour. That means 20 percent off."

You could only buy seven grams worth of marijuana, per dispensary, per day. We had a long weekend ahead of us, and drugs would be readily available, so we didn't overextend. We just got our Friday-night starter kit: two fat joints of a potent sativa called Blue Bastard, a gram of a really sweet-smelling sativa-dominant hybrid called Flo, and the tourist specialty of the house—a Skywalker OG cross joint, two joints sewn together into a paper cross. It burned from three ends.

"Five people would be flying off that thing," the budtender said.

"We'll take it!" we said, eagerly.

He put our purchases into a plastic bag with the Cannasseur logo on it. The bag sealed shut with a zipper, which then got inserted into a plastic clip. By law, all weed sold in Colorado has to be in childproof containers.

Some shops take care of this by distributing their goods in pill bottles. Others use these special sealed envelopes and charge clueless tourists up to twenty dollars for them. Cannasseur only tacked on a three-dollar bag surcharge. The zipper broke the first time it opened.

Regardless, we had plenty of excellent pot that we'd obtained legally at a reasonable market price, plus tax.

We drove a few miles to a restaurant, loaded a bowl of Flo, walked behind a dumpster, and each horked several massive hits of potent industrial-grade Cannabis sativa.

"Oh, crap," Rich said. "I have to sit down."

"Okay," I said.

"I can't feel my legs."

He started fanning his face in a panic.

"Dude," I said. "You're fine. You've smoked weed thousands of times before. This is just a little stronger."

I talked Rich off the ledge. He took a few breaths and chilled. Then we went inside, and each ate an enormous helping of huevos rancheros. It tasted damn good. Rich still couldn't feel his legs. But I could feel mine. They felt like freedom.

● ● ●

The headline of a short article in the Jan. 7, 2014 edition of *The Pueblo Chieftain* announced, "Local hotel smoker-friendly." In the article, the manager of the Microtel off I-25 said that it was opening up nine of its sixty-three rooms to marijuana smokers. "We figure people are going to do it whether we let them or not," she said.

Two nights before we left, I called the Microtel.

"I would like to order one of your marijuana-friendly hotel rooms," I said.

"You mean our smoking rooms?" said the person on the other end of the line.

"Yes," I said.

"That would be no problem," she said.

We arrived at the Microtel after 9:00 p.m. on a Friday with plenty of legal weed in our Cannasseur-sealed bag. Four preteens chased one another up and down the halls. A guy walked through carrying a plastic milk-crate full of Christian textbooks. This was the most ordinary place in America. Except that you could get high in your room here, legally and without breaking any of the rules on the back of the hotel room's door, before you hit the breakfast buffet.

There *was* a problem. Every smoking room was taken. The dinner rush had sucked them all away.

"But we reserved a marijuana room," I said. "Ahead of time. Is the whole hotel sold out?"

"Oh, no," the clerk said. "Just the smoking rooms. There's always a ton of demand."

She called her manager. A couple minutes passed, then she handed me a key.

"A lot of times we'll just convert another room into a smoking room," she said. "If the cleaning staff gives you a hard time, just tell them you had our permission."

"Will do," I said. "I appreciate it."

"Of course."

It became clear to me that the smoking rooms were no afterthought. Marijuana addicts like me were out-of-state VIP guests at this Microtel.

"A lot of professional people like you are coming here to smoke," she said to me. "It's not very ghetto."

That last comment made me uncomfortable. What does it matter if something is "ghetto" or not? But modest racism aside, I'd arrived at a hotel, in America, where I could get stoned. And nobody could say a goddamn thing.

We opened the door. Our room was clean, but small, and very depressing. It looked like a place where junkies got high. There were two queen beds and no closet. Rich, thinking like a true stoner, went into the bathroom, grabbed a towel, and stuffed it under the door.

"You don't have to do that, man," I said, while loading a bowl. "We have nothing to hide."

"I've gotten high in hundreds of hotel rooms like this," he said. "It's habit."

I did agree to open the window, though.

We got stoned for a while. Then we got more stoned. Soon, we got stoned again, and then a little bit more stoned and then we went to bed. It had been a long travel day, and we were old dads. We needed to preserve our energy.

We woke up early, before 7:00 a.m., excited as five-year-olds on Christmas morning. I opened the curtains to see our digs in daylight. On one side of the interstate was a Taco Bell. On the other side, a steel mill sent depressing plumes of smoke into the ash-gray sky. The Shire, this was not. But we had lots of weed, and we were going to buy lots more.

"Spark the Blue Bastard," I said.

I smoked a joint in bed, still wearing my pajamas.

Pueblo, we quickly learned, isn't much of a vacation spot. It's a semi-depressed steel town of slightly more than 100,000 residents, in the middle of some of the grayest, least-attractive landscapes in North America. It has few good bars and no real nightlife. The city's major claim to fame is "The Slopper," a cheeseburger smothered in hot chili sauce that has been eaten several times on The Food Network.

"It's like you drove to Texas for vacation, but ended up in Waco," Rich said. "No one goes on vacation to Waco."

We went to a couple more dispensaries, got a tour of Cannasseur's grow facilities, and drove around high as mockingbirds. Soon, though, desperate for scenery, we hauled our asses over to Colorado Springs. We walked around The Garden of the Gods, surrounded by families taking in its touristy splendor, looking for a hidden place where we could duck away from the wind and spark our Skywalker OG. The gods would have wanted me to get baked.

We lasted fewer than forty-eight hours in Colorado. Rich and I drove home on a Sunday morning. We'd seen about as much of Pueblo as we wanted, and neither of us had any interest in spending one more second in that Microtel.

"Besides," he said, "it's not like I'm never coming back."

He had plenty of resources. Soon after, he rented a condo in the mountains with some rich friends and did the Colorado experience right. I'd already planned two separate trips myself in the following six months. Now that I had a taste of the freedom, I was going to keep getting freer and freer, as often as I could, even if it killed me.

Which it almost did.

WHAT A DOPE

I first smoked pot in 1985 when I was fifteen years old, a sophomore in high school. At that time, I was busy emulating Alex P. Keaton, Michael J. Fox's *Family Ties* character, competing hard for every award and prestigious academic society, kissing every butt I could so I could be a High Achiever. But on the weekends, I often found myself in bad situations. It was an era of questionable but often awesome music, and untrustworthy drugs.

One night, my friend Gary and I went to a party in an apartment complex near my high school. Rush and Motley Crüe were on the turntable, beer was in the fridge and on the shag carpet, and a giant dirty bong sat on the coffee table. No responsible adult got anywhere near the proceedings.

No one was there to supervise me or initiate me—no friend, older sibling, or trusted ally. I took a nasty rip off that filthy bong and felt the burn through my entire chest. I writhed around on the couch, coughing, smoke spilling out of my ears. And then I took another hit. I sank back into the couch, completely baked.

The Yellow Pages sat next to me on a side table. *That book is stupid,* I thought. *I'm gonna destroy it.* For the next hour, or what seemed like it, I tried to tear the Yellow Pages in half. Not page by page, or a few pages at a time, but the *entire book at once.* I had the ability; I had the concentration. Like He-Man himself, I had the power.

After midnight, I staggered into my house. Someone, probably not someone sober, had given me a ride home. The front door was right by my parents' bedroom. My mother emerged, looking concerned.

I collapsed to the floor, weeping. Most likely, I'd been drinking as well.

"*I'm sorry, Mommy!*" I cried. "*I'm sorry!*"

Nothing particularly bad had happened to me that night. I'd smoked weed and had tried to tear a phone book in half. If it had ended that way, it would just be a funny story. I've always told it like that. But the real story ended with me in the hall, sobbing, slathered in my own mucus, until Mom finally persuaded me to go to bed.

My pathetic reaction should have indicated I was no chill stoner dude. I couldn't just chalk it all up to skanky '80s ditch weed. Marijuana and I were a bad mix that should be avoided.

For a while, I remembered this. In college, I slacked off slightly as I discovered people who made zines and listened to bands in basements, but still forged ahead in high-success mode. One night during my freshman year, the cool long-haired hippie anti-apartheid guy (who these days is a bald Manhattan attorney defending fraud and RICO cases) had a bong in his dorm room. I took a big rip and coughed so hard I vomited into my hands. That was it for marijuana and me in college, though I did trip balls on mushrooms once while performing the role of "Animal" in a live festival-day performance of an episode of *The Muppet Show.*

I'd tried pot twice. The first time I turned into an insane baby, and the second time I barfed into my hands. Naturally, I ended up getting high every day of my adult life. I not only became psychologically dependent on it, but I also bragged about that fact to the point where I became a leading outspoken public advocate for its use. I never publicly extolled love for a human as much as I crowed about how much I loved marijuana.

In my twenties, I had a job as a reporter in Chicago for a free weekly newspaper. Even though it paid a full-time salary, it still felt more like freelancing. I had basically no deadlines, no quotas, and no desk in any office. It was the start of an adult life where I stumbled into not making a ton of money, but basically having unlimited free time to do whatever I wanted. No one really cared what I was doing, or when. That's a perfect recipe for a stoner's life. I started getting high for real. Those were casual bohemian days of late-night apartment parties, dancing, and long, serious conversations about Big Ideas. Soon I was getting high several times a week. Unlike booze, pot didn't leave me with a whopping hangover the next day—just a little brain-fuzz around the edges, which I could easily alleviate by getting stoned again. Often.

I met Regina in 1997. She placed a personal ad in the newspaper where I worked. It read, *Wayward Southern belle seeks single gentleman with penchant for scatological humor.* Several friends pointed me toward the ad, but I'd already answered it. And within a few weeks, we were together. When I responded to her ad, I was really into weed, but not as into weed as I would be by the time we got married three years later. She only smoked with me occasionally; Regina is a good Protestant girl from Tennessee, so she prefers a moderate nip of bourbon, and a slightly-less-moderate amount of gin.

I was beginning my exciting journey to becoming famous, in an independent-book-publishing sort of way. Someone I went to college with went to high school with a guy named

Dave Eggers, which wasn't a big deal when I was in college, but it was a much bigger deal when he suddenly became the editor of *Might* magazine in San Francisco, which was kind of trendy. I wrote a few pieces for him then. And then he transformed into the hottest writer in Brooklyn and started publishing *McSweeney's*, a literary magazine and website that people who read literary magazines and websites enjoyed. You had to be there, and I was.

I'd been reading little satirical pieces at open-mic nights in Chicago, parodies of writing by men who were more famous and successful than I was. They went over pretty well, but they went over *really* well when I sent them to Eggers, when he published them as the first article in the first issue of *McSweeney's*, and when I became a popular writer on the *McSweeney's* humor website. I started calling myself The Greatest Living American Writer. It was not a modest debut.

Eggers decided to start publishing books. The Greatest Living American Writer was first through the gates of glory. *The Neal Pollack Anthology of American Literature* got a full-page review in the *New York Times*, and, in the fall of 2000, *Rolling Stone* named me the Hot Writer of the Millennium in 2000. I didn't get rich, but I did do a lot of interviews. I toured around promoting myself, reading in front of audiences that, today, I realize were absurdly large for a first-time satirical fiction writer. I opened for They Might Be Giants at the Bowery Ballroom. Not my band. Just me reading poetry. Somehow, I was a rock star. And as a rock star, people started offering me drugs. I took them all.

For the next fifteen-plus years, my life was a nonstop marijuana binge. I ate it and smoked it and vaped it off a beautiful desktop set called the Silver Surfer. Long before battery-powered vape pens appeared, I used a blown-glass mouthpiece attached to a rubber tube with another glass piece on the end. It was a ridiculous ritual, given that the average stoner now carries around in their pocket enough concentrated THC to tranquilize a moose.

I got high in bedrooms and bathrooms and alleys and basements, in hotels and restaurants, on boats and trains and in cars. I flew stoned from coast to coast and around the world, getting baked with writers, artists, musicians, award-winning actors, yoga teachers, random slackers, and whoever else I could find. If you had weed, you were my friend. From college students to old men, it was no country for non-stoners. It never really occurred to me that I was an addict.

A MEMBER OF THE ROCK STAR POET LITERARY ELITE

In 2002, I should have been flying on the natural high of people actually being interested in me; instead, I just did drugs. I was on a twenty-city tour for the paperback edition of the anthology, an insanely unprofitable proposition considering that book sold maybe 10,000 copies. After an appearance at an independent bookstore in Madison, I went back to some grad student's apartment and got high. They made a batch of special brownies for me. I ate one and took two for the road.

The next day I boarded a flight for Dallas where I was to meet with Dave Eggers, who'd originally published my book and unleashed my ego onto the world. The Dallas Museum of Art had booked us to appear at a reading and discussion. He got the gig because he was legitimately famous and people wanted to hear what he had to say. I was there because I lived in Texas and because I was his amusing sidekick. They paid me $5,000. Five thousand dollars! To sit in a chair and do literary chat. That's how much big-time writers get paid to appear at art museums and big public theaters. Sometimes they get more. One shouldn't squander such opportunities. But I squandered mine.

Three hours before the event, I scarfed one of the brownies in my hotel room. Then I got into the bathtub and ate another one.

I arrived at the event flying higher than any Mercury astronaut. In the Green Room, I shoved grapes into my mouth and pretended to be a chipmunk. My eyes were as wide as commemorative plates. I was fat and pale and sweaty. Onstage, I bumbled through my reading. When Eggers read, I snuffled dismissively and slumped down in my chair like a disdainful greaser in *Blackboard Jungle.* The question-and-answer period was an obnoxious session of more disdainful dismissing and eye-rolling. Eggers was getting annoyed with me. He said something. I responded "whatever." Then he said something else. I dropped lower in my chair and blew my lips together. Literary events do tend to be stupid and pretentious. Who cares what writers have to say about anything? But, you know, they were paying me $5,000. Did I not realize that most writers don't get paid $5,000 to pontificate? That's a lot of money now and it was an *enormous* amount of money then. I could have at least been polite.

After my reading, I went back to the hotel and took a bath. I had seven special cookies in a plastic wrapper. Fuck it, I thought, and ate three of them as I lowered myself into the water. Afterward, some guy I'd never met before held a huge house party in my honor. There were drugs available. I smoked them, and then ate the rest of the cookies. I hung out in the kitchen with strangers on the off chance they'd tell me

I was awesome. For me, that was the whole point of being a writer. Dave Eggers, on the other hand, had already completed his adolescence, so he'd moved beyond that impulse. Eggers made a brief appearance at the party, the kind of thing he'd soon stop doing as his star continued to rise and he devoted his life to public service and literary excellence. I, on the other hand, would probably come over to your house for dinner tonight if you asked me.

I lay in a hammock, my tongue lolling out of my mouth.

"Are you okay?" he asked.

"I am nifty," I said.

"Listen," he said. "I want things to be more straightforward from now on."

"Blurgh," I said.

Only the next morning, doubled over in an airport bathroom stall, did I understand. Dave had broken up with me! Not a problem, I figured. I'd just score those multi-thousand-dollar speaking gigs without him.

Those dried up almost immediately. Dave and I remained friends. I even went to his wedding in San Francisco. Jonathan Richman performed a special song. But then a year or so later, in the midst of a self-promotional push, I wrote a piece where I quoted Eggers as telling me, back at the beginning, that we were "entering a new era of literary celebrity," and that I needed to push it while I had some heat. He did say that, but he also didn't like to admit that he'd done anything professionally on purpose. It was all magically serendipitous that he ended up co-writing a movie with Spike Jonze and having his books made into films starring Tom Hanks. None of that matters now, and he deserves all his success. But at the time, he was very pissed off, wrote some nasty things about me on the Internet, and cut me out of the family entirely.

Years later, when I sobered up, I was thinking about making some Ninth Step amends to Eggers. I got his email address and thought about dropping him a line. But I never did. Maybe this counts as my amends. He was hanging around with Barack Obama and various other saints in human form. If I'd just sobered up, maybe I'd be friends with Malala right now. I'm guessing she doesn't do drugs.

● ● ●

I wrote another book, and then another. My time as a member of the literary elite led me to think that I was a rock star. I wrote a novel, *Never Mind the Pollacks*, making fun of the rock critic Greil Marcus's obsession with the rock critic Lester Bangs, and persuaded a publisher to release this novel. It sold 4,000 copies, which is pretty good for a novel about rock critics, but not exactly rock star numbers. To promote this book, I started a punk-rock band called The Neal Pollack Invasion, even though I played no musical instruments, couldn't read music, and, frankly, didn't even like music all that much. Somehow, I persuaded a record label to release this album, which included songs with titles like "New York City (Is a Pile of Shit)" and "I Wipe My Ass on Your Novel." I also got my publisher to pay for a rock tour. We played dive clubs across the country, on bills that included more famous bands like Broken Social Scene, and also played at the now-gone Virgin Megastore in New York's Union Square. And I appeared on *The Daily Show with Jon Stewart*, which played a clip of "New York City Is a Pile of Shit." After our tour, the record label went bankrupt, leaving all copies of our CDs trapped in a warehouse in Lawrence, Kansas for more than a decade. All this is true.

Most importantly, being in a rock band gave me many opportunities to get stoned. Everyone knows it's impossible to make music without the help of drugs. My main musical collaborator liked weed as much as I did. We got high before every rehearsal and also after every rehearsal. There was no way I could perform unless I was stoned, and I definitely needed to be stoned to come down from the excitement of the show. When I recorded an album on a laptop in my lead guitarist's apartment living room, I got high between every take, sometimes during a take. Nothing amused me more than blowing a big puff of smoke into the microphone right when I started singing. By doing drugs and singing rock 'n' roll, I was truly busting new cultural ground.

Meanwhile, the John Adams Institute of Amsterdam invited me to be the American representative to the annual National Poetry Day of Holland. Because I'd never actually published a poem in English, I was a somewhat odd selection for this honor. In my home country, I generally performed my spoken-word parodies in front of a dozen people or fewer in the back rooms of independent bookstores, but in the Low Countries, several thousand people would soon witness my questionable act in grand opera houses and cavernous, acoustically generous concert halls built for acts like Oasis and Blur. Years before he sobered up himself, Oscar, my Dutch publisher, thought he might be able to cash in on this situation.

We packaged pieces from my first book with some political satire and about a dozen poems all translated into Dutch, and sold it under the title *Neal Pollack's Undying Love for the Citizens of Holland (and also Belgium)*. The book cover featured me wearing a Homestead Grays cap backward, an Allen Iverson jersey, $5 sunglasses and a goatee, with my arms crossed and looking like a failed auditionee for a Beastie Boys tribute band. I'm still not sure why the John Adams Institute invited me as opposed to, say, John Ashbery, or any other person in the United States who actually writes poetry, but it was a free plane ticket and an opportunity to get high in Amsterdam.

"Do you have to do this?" Regina asked.

"It would be a great insult to the John Adams Institute if I didn't," I said.

"We have a three-month-old baby," she said. "Don't you care about him at all?"

"Of course I do," I said. "I care about him more than anything in the world. But I still want to go to Amsterdam."

"You just want to go to Amsterdam so you can smoke pot," she said.

"That's not true," I said.

She looked at me, arms crossed.

"Okay," I said. "It *is* true. But that's not the only reason."

Even though it was.

For twenty-four hours in Amsterdam, I was a responsible representative of my country. Oscar had set up some interviews for me with high-powered outlets like a monthly Jewish newspaper from Rotterdam. Also, as part of the National Poetry Day celebration, the Institute had assigned all the participants to write a fable and to teach a workshop about fables to a local high school class. I hadn't written a fable since I was eight, and it showed; in a couple of hours I slapped out a lame animal parable about tolerance, based on the recent assassination of Dutch prime ministerial candidate Pim Fortuyn, about whom I knew nothing. Then I taught my class and chose, as the organizers had instructed, the "best" student to give a presentation that evening. She would compete against the other students from the other classes for a prize. Up until fifteen minutes after my lecture ended, I was sober.

As I walked out into the late afternoon, I had three hours before I had to present my poetry in a public performance. I decided it was the perfect time to get high. Amsterdam's coffee shops held no mystery for me. I'd visited many times and since I basically did nothing else in the city besides visit art museums or eat cheese, I'd more or less memorized a stoner's walking tour that would be the envy of the most experienced Cannabis Cup judge.

When I next looked at my watch, two hours and fifteen minutes had passed in a magnificent haze of high-octane legal weed and herbal tea. I'd enjoyed conversations with a one-armed Nigerian taxi driver and an anthropology professor for a low-rent Midwestern community college who'd just emerged from a two-day mushroom trip in his hotel room. I stepped onto a major thoroughfare, full of confidence in myself as a professional and as a dad. I pulled a picture of Elijah out of my wallet and thought:

I love my son so much. Look at him! He's so beautiful. Life with him is going to be a wonder. I'm the luckiest man in the world! Now, what happened to the Keizergracht? This is one of the main canals ringing the center of the city. It's fairly easy to find if you're sober. But I was not.

To my right, I saw one of Amsterdam's many "smart shops." Now mostly banned, particularly from selling magic mushrooms, in the early 2000s these shops were at their height. I walked in, briefly pondered a display of homegrown peyote, bought a packet of some sort, and swallowed two pills with a gulp of water.

By the time I arrived at the venue to perform, my lips felt like sausages. Oscar gave me a conspiratorial grin.

"How are you *feeling?*" he said.

I couldn't tell him that at the moment I was imagining that my eyes had popped out of their sockets, shot forward ten feet attached by thin ligaments, wrapped themselves around my head, and reinserted themselves in new sockets that had opened up just above my eyebrows. He wouldn't have understood. So instead I said, "Oh, fine."

I was second on that evening's program. My opening act was Gerrit Komrij, the poet laureate of Holland. He wore mostly black and read in Dutch. This gave me a lot of time to ponder the fact that my legs were slowly melting into the floor. I wondered how I'd make it up to the podium without them, particularly since the rest of my body was slowly filling up with oatmeal. When the poet laureate of Holland cut his reading short because he had a train to catch, the emcee introduced me as our "distinguished American visitor." When I took the podium, my body dripped with sweat.

"Good evening, people of the Netherlands," I said. "My name is Neal Pollack. And I am the Greatest Living American Writer."

With that, I lifted a pitcher of water off the podium and dumped it over my head.

Oscar and his friends seemed to think it was funny, even if the rest of the crowd didn't. This encouraged me to continue. We were on the eve of the Iraq invasion; as I sat there not listening to the poet laureate of Holland, I'd decided to deliver a monologue of pure patriotic bluster to parody the misguided war fever that was currently gripping the United States.

"I stand here representing the greatest country in the history of the world, the beacon of democracy to oppressed people everywhere. Our enemies tremble in the face of our awesome military might and our international system of secret prisons that are accountable to no one. Our allies feel safe and comfortable under our broad protective wings. All hail the United States of America, where literature kicks big ass!"

A man in the back of the hall rose, shouted, "You will be punished!" and stormed out of the hall. I later learned that he was the *Iraqi* representative to National Poetry Day. Apparently, you don't appreciate irony when the U.S. is about to invade your country. Later, the event organizers had me email the Iraqi poet to try and heal the rift, but it only got worse. He wrote, "You are complicit in the crimes of your President, as are all the American people." I replied, "Don't blame me, I didn't want this war." Thus ended an historic epistolary exchange.

The rest of the evening was a mix. My student from the fable class gave a great presentation and won the prize, but later, during a discussion panel, I compared a German poet to Hitler and accused the moderator of asking the "stupidest questions of all time." I don't recall the question, but it probably wasn't that stupid. When someone in the audience asked me what advice I'd give to young people who wanted to be writers, I said, "It doesn't matter what you say. If you say it loud enough, and for long enough, eventually people will pay attention."

"Well," the moderator said. "I'm certain we will now live our lives according to Mr. Pollack's wise advice."

Afterward, my prizewinning student came up to me with her parents.

"Thank you," her father said. "You have really inspired my daughter."

"I have a son," I said. "So I understand." The next time I visited Amsterdam, I was a guest on a show for the improv group Boom Chicago. Again, I did huge quantities of legal drugs, at a time when this couldn't happen in the States. My head felt like it puffed to three times its normal size. My eyes went wide and I dripped with sweat. I thought I was super-cute. When the show ended, I stood center stage and shouted, "THANK YOU, EUROPE!" Then I pulled down my pants, exposing my dick to several hundred people. I didn't have an "artistic" reason for doing this. The drugs had taken away every inhibition. Like a six-year-old at the park or a sixty-seven-year-old flasher, I saw no reason why I shouldn't show everyone my privates. I did drugs, and out came the schlong.

Then it was 3:00 a.m. and I was in my hotel room. My breathing was raspy and shallow. I called home.

"How'd it go?" Regina asked.

I told her.

"Oh, Neal," she said.

"Why does this always happen to me?" I asked.

"I don't know," she said.

But the answer was: Because I was an addict.

A COOL STONER DAD

My wife got pregnant. This was a time for me to celebrate! With marijuana. I was determined to be a cool dad, and, to me, cool meant high. I was hanging around with guys younger than me, having a blast, horking huge plastic bags of vapor out of this one dude's volcano, driving around town stoned out of my wits. One night when Regina went into false labor, I was hanging out with these guys in a random apartment near the University of Texas, getting stoned with some college kids who liked my books. Very cool.

After my son Elijah was born, I continued getting stoned all the time. During those rare sixteen or seventeen hours a day that I had to myself, I'd slip around back of the house to load a bowl or two or three. One day I had to return books to the library, and I couldn't possibly do that errand without getting high. It was a nice sunny day outside—best enjoyed under the influence of marijuana, just like crummy weather days. I guzzled the Silver Surfer, then loaded my mini pipe in case I needed a touch-up while I was out.

I walked about three blocks before I decided that I needed to get more stoned. It was very windy out, so I had trouble lighting the pipe. I ducked into an alley and squatted behind a dumpster, scorching my thumb trying to ignite the pipe. It occurred to me that crouching behind a garbage can in an alley to get a fix is something that a junkie might do. Occasionally, I'd have brief moments of conscience like that, but the thought quickly went away. I wasn't a *drug addict*; I just needed to smoke pot all day, every day.

As my son grew up, I kept getting high. In 2010, I contributed an essay to *The Pot Book: A Complete Guide to Cannabis*. Edited by Dr. Julie Holland, a physician and drug researcher, this pre-legalization volume brought together scientists, doctors, and philosophers to educate the public about marijuana. My voice was pretty much the least authoritative. But because I'd been so out and proud about my pot use, and because I wrote about it amusedly and unabashedly, she asked me to contribute.

The editor titled my essay "Pot, Parenting, and Outing Myself." It began with the charming and hilarious story of how I, at age thirty-five, purchased my beloved Silver Surfer desktop vaporizer and learned terms like "heat source," "mouthpiece," "whip," and "wand."

"It would be the greatest present I'd ever give myself," I wrote. "No more apple bongs for me. I had to consume my THC wisely. I was a dad now."

Looking back at that piece now, I'm ashamed and appalled at my selfishness and myopia. I wrote, "It never really occurred to me to give up weed just because I'd become a parent. If anything, parenthood meant that marijuana became a larger part of my life. Whereas before the boy's arrival I'd often leave the house after 9:00 p.m. for a party, or a bar, or a movie, now my social life has contracted. I have no money and all my friends are either parents, and therefore have no time for socializing, or single, and therefore have no time for socializing with parents . . . A hit off the Silver Surfer and a night of Turner Classic Movies often seems like an acceptable compromise."

I wrote in *The Pot Book*: "Anyone who says it's impossible to be a stoner and a parent has either never been a stoner, or never been a parent. Weed doesn't prevent me from being a good dad. I never forget anything. Playdates and birthday parties and swim lessons get arranged. Stuff gets bought. The kid takes his vitamins and I comb the dead skin out of his hair. I'm never neglectful. I'm always attentive and supportive. Sometimes I'm a little grumpy in the mornings, but I've always been a little grumpy in the mornings."

But I *did* forget things and I *was* occasionally neglectful. This was an era before streaming entertainment, when Netflix came in the mail. But it was just as easy to go to the video store, especially since we lived a block away from a place called I Love Video, which specialized in weird movies. One day, completely blasted, I drove the station wagon over to the video store and got a couple of DVDs. Then I went home and we watched them.

The next morning, I woke up and saw that the car wasn't in the driveway.

"Regina," I said. "I think someone stole our car."

"What?" she said.

It wasn't out of the question. We lived in a pretty high-crime neighborhood near the Interstate. People got their windows blasted out all the time, packages got stolen. I witnessed a prostitute killing a man by stabbing him through the heart with a coat hanger. So sure, our car could have been stolen.

"When was the last time you drove it?" she said.

"I took it to the video store and . . . oh shit."

I walked down the street. There was the car, in the parking lot of the video store. I'd just walked home high and left it there.

But I got away with it, like I got away with most things. I benefited from having no real job, a lot of free time, and especially a kind and patient and probably a little bit codependent spouse. You can be a good dad and smoke a little weed, just like you can be a good dad and have a beer now and then. But I wasn't smoking a little weed. I was high all the time. It was my dominant reality. I didn't deserve a medal because my son usually brushed his teeth.

While it's true that some stoner parents are great parents and some sober parents are lousy parents, it's also true that when drugs get involved, the parenting odds change. And when addiction gets involved, they change a lot.

The following section in my *Pot Book* piece strikes me as especially pathetic:

> I'm downplaying my marijuana use. Mostly, it doesn't come up, though there are occasional situations, like when I get a bag of the strong stuff and there's a stench in the house; my wife and I refer to the smell as "daddy's stinky tea," or, alternately, we tell him that that the dog got sprayed by a skunk.

> Then there was the time Elijah found a little pipe on the stairs one day and asked about it; I told him it was for a snowman. When he pointed out that there's no snow where we live, ever, I told him, "I'm mailing it to a friend so he can build a snowman with his kids."

> The other day, Elijah used the bathroom off my office because the other one was occupied. He spotted the Silver Surfer on the floor.

> "What's that, Daddy?" he asked.

> "Nothing," I said. "Just something Daddy uses to help him with his breath."

"Good," he said. "Your breath stinks sometimes."

"Yeah, well, so does yours," I said.

At the time that seemed adorable to me, but now it just feels sad. Ah, those tender memories of dad's weed breath! I was smoking a lot of pot, but I was about to start smoking even more. It happens when a marijuana addict moves to California.

● ● ●

I wrote a book about being a cool stoner dad. It was called *Alternadad*, and I really thought that made me an even *cooler* stoner dad. It all starts to get pretty meta, but this was my life. To tell it any other way would be disingenuous or nonsensical. *Alternadad* seemed like a hot commodity at the time. It got optioned by Warner Brothers Pictures. They hired the comedian Dana Gould to write a screenplay. I was going to be a very rich and famous stoner dad. It was time. Like Thanos, I was inevitable.

Within weeks of arriving, I went to a nondescript office in Beverly Hills, where a handsome man with a blond pompadour and a lot of teeth sat behind a cheap desk in an office with no books on the shelves and no medical degrees on the wall. This was my "doctor." He asked me what my "condition" was. I told him anxiety and depression. He took my blood pressure with a child's toy, then signed my medical card.

Marijuana was the only constant in Los Angeles. I was high at the poker table and the ballpark, watching TV, writing, going to meetings, eating dinner, lunch, and, on the rare occasions when I got up in the morning, breakfast. Thinking that I was breaking new gonzo ground, I smoked pot outside a synagogue, and also *inside* a synagogue.

I brought marijuana candy to my son's preschool fundraiser. Within minutes, the tent at the silent auction reeked of weed. The candy was that powerful. It would have gotten me arrested at most airports, or if I were black.

"What you got there?" asked another dad. I opened up my vintage tuxedo jacket to reveal a silver packet of "Reefer's Peanut Butter Cups."

Our rental house stank of weed; so did the next one, as well as all the different houses we rented in an attempt to outrun the fact that things weren't going as well as I'd hoped. I was probably spending too much money on weed, but we were basically spending too much money on *everything*. We had no business being there.

I smoked in hammocks and hot tubs, at the beach and at the top of Griffith Park. About three years in, when it was becoming abundantly clear that my only legacy in Hollywood was going to be complaining about not getting paid, my manager said to me, "Maybe you should quit smoking pot." *Screw you,* I thought. *Get me a job.* But boy was she right. I wasn't missing meetings and I made phone calls. But I wasn't working. Mostly, I was smoking weed and dreaming about hitting it big. I wasn't going to hit it big, or at least not any bigger than I did. But there would always be more weed.

In April 2011, just a few months before I drove my 1998 Nissan Sentra away from California in shame and disillusionment, I published a sad little article titled called "Confessions of a Prominent Pothead" on an addiction-recovery website called *The Fix.* In the piece, I tried to diagnose whether or not I was addicted to marijuana, using the seven addiction criteria of the American Psychiatric Association. Looking back on it now, the piece was a pathetic rationalization of my addictive behavior. "Sometimes I get a headache and am grouchy the day after using pot," I wrote, "but I sometimes get a headache and am grouchy regardless." Very cute, but I *didn't* write, "I overslept and missed a breakfast meeting in Santa Monica because I was getting high until 2:00 a.m. And then I did the same thing the next week."

Then there was this bit:

6. Use of the drug interferes with engagement in important social, recreational, and work-related activities. There were times, in the past, when I was getting into bar fights and yelling at people for no reason. I was also drinking then, sometimes a lot, or at least more than I should. So I stopped drinking alcohol, other than the occasional beer or glass of wine. That immediately improved my sleep, my work, my fun, and my relationships with my wife and family and friends. I determined that alcohol, consumed to excess, is unequivocally evil, and combining it with marijuana can be incredibly dangerous. Pot by itself doesn't have the same sinister overtones.

Maybe not. But *writing about pot in those terms* does. I concluded the essay with this peachy anecdote:

A couple of years ago, a friend from up north brought me a fat bag of Humboldt County homegrown, a real-life version of *Pineapple Express*. I started vaporizing it immediately, and then I started taking it with me to smoke, and then I started eating it in big clumps, because I had so much in that bag that I really couldn't even begin to make a dent. I got higher than I ever had in my life—a deep, soul-sucking high that, after about two weeks, began to enervate me until I couldn't get off the floor some days, so then I smoked some more, and it got worse. I found myself sinking into the deepest depression I'd ever felt. No amount of yoga helped. My Wellbutrin prescription seemed to fail entirely. I hated myself utterly and forever. Finally, I came to terms with the fact that the weed was doing this to me. Maybe I was an addict, I thought, and I had to stop. At last, I'd bottomed out. So I sealed up the bag, only opening it to give it away to people, one pill bottle-full at a time.

But then, as I wrote, things got better when I tried a different strain of weed, which made me feel "better." "The odd biochemical disruption of the previous mutant strain of marijuana passed entirely," I said. "That's what makes weed different from something like, say, Scotch. When you drink, you pretty much know what you're going to get. But marijuana, like coffee, tea, or cheese, can vary so much in flavor and effect. It can be cheap or expensive, strong or mellow, harmful or friendly. One strain can ruin you, while another can delight."

I concluded the essay with: "When you add it all up, I score somewhere between borderline addict and regular stoner. So am I a ganja fiend who's just trying to justify his addiction? Maybe. Probably. I'm not sure. This is going to have to go to the lab for further analysis. As the Magic 8-Ball says, in what appears to be a coded message to stoners, "Reply Hazy. Try Again Later."

In retrospect, the piece was me saying, "I can stop any time I want." Like a true addict, I was garrulous, flippant, and self-justifying. A normal person would read a story about a guy smoking so much weed that he couldn't get off the floor and think: *That guy has a problem.* But to me, the logical solution was that I just needed better pot. Being constantly stoned in Hollywood may work fine for Snoop Dogg and Seth Rogen. But it sure didn't work for me.

THE LONG NIGHT OF MY TRIVIA SOUL

I played a regular pub-trivia night in Los Angeles called Booze Clues. One night, my usual team, which always lost, couldn't make the game, so I played with a couple of friends from out of town: a poetry professor and a scholar of Jewish studies, both super-smart, both with broad intellects. The three of us did great.

We tied for first with another team. The host told the teams to send up one member each. I'd assembled our squad, so they sent me. Our host read the tiebreaking question.

"Name the first rock star," he said, "whose penis Cynthia Plaster Caster sculpted to begin her famous collection."

If there were ever a trivia question tailor-made for me, it was this one. Cynthia Plaster Caster was a longtime fixture of Chicago's underground music scene, who got her name from making plaster casts out of rock stars' dicks. I'd hung out on the fringes of that scene in the '90s, and knew Cynthia pretty well, though I never got casted. But she and I *had* licked Fireball shots off the disgusting laminate tabletops at the legendary Bucket O'Suds bar on the night it closed. So I knew the answer before the host was even done speaking.

"Jimi Hendrix," I said immediately.

The host looked legitimately surprised.

"That is correct," he said.

I raised my hands in triumph. That was my first glorious taste of trivia victory. More, please. Like Veruca Salt—also a band from the Chicago rock scene, and also a common trivia answer—I wanted it all. I wanted to answer a question about an Oompa-Loompa *now*.

A few years later, in January 2013, my former neighbor in Austin posted on his Facebook wall that the *Jeopardy!* online test was coming up soon. He'd won a game of *Jeopardy!* the previous year, and he wanted his friends to have the same opportunity for happiness.

It's hard to say why I hadn't taken the *Jeopardy!* test earlier. I just hadn't. But then I did, and I knew most of the answers. About a month after that, I got this email:

> **Congratulations!** You have been selected for a follow-up appointment at an upcoming *Jeopardy!* contestant search for the San Antonio area, exclusively for those who successfully passed the online test. This is the next step in becoming a *Jeopardy!* contestant. We have reserved the following appointment for you:
>
> **When: Wednesday, March 13th**
>
> **Time: 3:00 pm**
>
> **Where: San Antonio, TX**
>
> You must **RSVP** *within two business days* of receipt of this email to secure your place in the audition.

I responded within two business *minutes*, with this highly neurotic email:

> Hello! I'm very excited to audition for *Jeopardy!*
> However, I do have a major conflict at that specific
> time. I'm in a rock band, and we're booked to play
> a showcase at 7:30 that night during the South by
> Southwest music festival in Austin. It's about ninety
> minutes from San Antonio to Austin with no traffic,
> so we'd be cutting it pretty close to get back for the big
> show. If I could have an earlier Wednesday audition
> time, even noon or 1:00 p.m., that would make my
> situation a lot easier. Let me know if you can make
> the change, and please feel free to call the number
> above or email me at this address at any time so we
> can arrange something. Thank you so much for the
> opportunity!

As it turned out, my band's "big show" ended up being attended by exactly three people, but *Jeopardy!* accommodated me and moved my appointment up to 11:30 a.m. Soon after, they sent this email:

> Congratulations! We are happy to confirm your
> appointment to participate in the full audition
> for *Jeopardy!*. That will consist of playing a "mock
> version" of *Jeopardy!* to assess your game-playing
> skills, a short personality interview, and being re-
> tested with a new 50-question test. If you pass all
> the requirements to become a contestant you will be
> entered into the contestant pool for one year. <u>However
> even though you pass the test, we cannot guarantee
> that you will be invited to do the show.</u>

If I passed the online test, I figured I'd pass the written one, too. As it turned out, they were more or less the same test, or at least the same type of test, and I had no trouble.

All those years of reading *The World Almanac and Book of Facts* alone in my bedroom as a child had finally paid some dividends. At last, I would cash in for memorizing *The Last Dog on the White House Lawn*.

The "short personality interview" took place in a modest conference room at the Westin. In the *Jeopardy!* universe, where the majority of contestants, given the opportunity to share one thing about themselves, say stuff like, "I proposed to my wife on a ship"; "I collect sports memorabilia"; "I went hiking on vacation"; or "I named my cat after you, Alex," my angle of "I'm a yoga-teaching novelist who drives race cars and fronts a rock band" seemed pretty solid.

The sample game, on the other hand, was actually kind of hard. I had trouble buzzing in. The contestant coordinators gave me some advice: wait until you see a light flash on the board. *Then* you buzz. I still didn't do particularly well. But I got in a few times, answered some questions correctly and with confidence, and I felt pretty good about my chances.

Somehow I knew I was going to be invited to do the show; I was ready for whatever came my way, I told myself. This was a lark, I told myself, a notch on the belt of experience. I should have been anxious, but I wasn't. My demeanor brimmed with false bravado.

But then, a few weeks later, *Jeopardy!* actually called. I'd not only been cast, but I'd been cast for the first week of taping for the upcoming season. If I could make it to Los Angeles in late August, I could be on the show. Suddenly, a funny side gig became a deadly serious mission.

For all my confidence and bragging, I really needed to win on *Jeopardy!* My five-year attempt to make it big in the TV and movie business in Los Angeles had ended in miserable failure. In the middle of the worst economic crisis of modern times, my wife and son and I had limped back to Austin in a 1998 Nissan Sentra with a five-figure credit card debt, no prospects, and very little hope. Though Regina had found a part-time job and I'd found a few freelance gigs, we still hadn't entirely recovered. We were living in an outrageously-priced and semi-terrifying rental house with sagging ceilings, peeling paint, and a furnace closet full of rodent droppings. Every day, I showered in a dark corner that had been hastily tiled, my head pressed against the smeared brown grout, wondering how the hell I was going to pull myself out of this mess. *Jeopardy!* would be my last best hope to rejoin the middle class. A trivia game show, though not the one that *usually* offered its contestants a lifeline, was giving me the opportunity to escape my mundane reality by winning some serious cash. I was going to do this big-time. It wasn't exactly the best plan, but it was a plan nonetheless.

More than the money, though, I wanted the glory. I found myself wandering stoned around midlife like a kid lost in a mall. But I was determined to not become the sad little man with broken dreams, faking a grin while the real winner got the adulation. The cameras would close in on my face. I would be the star.

Even though I'd already achieved quite a bit in my life, it hadn't been enough. I wanted more attention, more validation, more acknowledgment that I was smart and good and cool and awesome, not the weak little kid getting bullied at the dining-room table by my grandfather and his friends, not the smart-mouth preadolescent wiener getting beaten up on the playground by two guys named Cory because he'd been named Student of the Month. Your typical *Jeopardy!* contestant is an educated person with some nerdy hobbies, but I also brought all my sweaty, neurotic, attention-seeking addict's behavior to the scene. It was more than just a game-show appearance. In my mind, I was going to claw myself up from the pits of hell. I would be a champion at game shows, and at life, and I would die knowing that I was the best at something.

A training montage ensued.

How, you're asking, does one *train* to appear on a quiz show? Well, the answer is, you do it the same as how you'd train to take part in any endeavor that requires extreme physical and mental endurance: through hard, disciplined, and merciless effort. I was going to be on television, possibly more than once, and I wanted to go in looking my best. So I adopted a protein-rich, low-carb, basically snack-and-sweet-free diet. I ramped up my already frequent yoga practice, doing up to two hours a day of pushups, arm balances, and inversions, supplemented with twenty to thirty minutes of focused meditation. I did it every day, even on Sunday. When I wasn't going to public classes, I practiced at home. I stopped drinking, save for an occasional glass of red wine. Most notably, I stopped smoking, vaping, otherwise inhaling, or eating marijuana, for the first time in nearly twenty years. I didn't touch the weed for *at least six weeks*. I wondered if there was a special reward for my extreme sacrifice. But even if there wasn't, my mind would be clean, my body strong and clear. I would transform myself into a holy avatar of trivia.

Into this sacred pot-free shell, I, the warrior monk of quiz, poured the molten lava of complete world knowledge. These days, *Jeopardy!* is a complete multimedia enterprise, with mobile apps, an Alexa app, and hundreds of archived episodes available on YouTube. While it will never be hip, exactly, it's modernized, substantially expanding its appeal. But at the time I appeared on the show, it had a barely viewed Twitter handle and a minimal social-media presence. It was still pretty much the show Grandma watched while eating her pudding. I had to do my *Jeopardy!* piecemeal.

Fortunately for me, there *was* the J! Archive. Maintained by a team of faceless saints, this website has collected all the clues from more or less every *Jeopardy!* game since the mid-1980s. The games are laid out like a classic *Jeopardy!* board grid, with all six categories going across and the dollar values rising as you travel from top to bottom. The board shows all the answers, and when you click on the answer, it reveals the question. For the seven of you who don't know, on *Jeopardy!* the question appears in the form of an answer, and the answer appears in the form of a question. This is part of a formula Merv Griffin devised many decades ago.

So there they were, all the *Jeopardy!* questions I could eat, thousands of nuggets of knowledge from the dawn of the Trebek era to the present. I sat in my tiny room with the cheap plastic blinds, drilling down, hard, running simulations for two or three hours straight, until my eyes crossed and my brain flatlined.

But it soon became clear that some types of categories showed more often than others. Though there's never a guarantee of what you're going to get on *Jeopardy!*, it helps to have a broad and semi-deep knowledge of American history, human biology, and Shakespeare. World capitals come as close as you can get to required material, and you'd better know your lakes, mountains, and rivers, too. Some stuff I could discard. A lot of the pop-culture ephemera from the nineties wouldn't fit into the modern game, with rare exceptions. Names of senators who were famous in 1987 were highly unlikely to appear. If I got a question about Phil Gramm or the girl who'd played the robot in *Small Wonder* (Tiffany something), well, more power to me, but I wasn't going to stake my claim on those.

Jeopardy! also has a strange bias toward "stuff Trebek likes." This means more Canadian geography than normal, a substantial amount of military history, and French homophones. It became apparent that, while answers did run pretty broad, material did repeat every 100 to 200 episodes or so. There was a decent chance you'd run into a question on "Captain Eddie Rickenbacker Day."

It became clear pretty fast where I was weak and needed extra study. Going any deeper on Literature, Sports, TV, Classic Hollywood, or American History would be a waste of time.

With great alacrity and fortitude, I declared my lexicological readiness to tackle all vocabulary-based categories. I went deep on Capitals, studied up on my geography, brushed up my Shakespeare. Some stuff, commonly asked on *Jeopardy!*, I didn't know at all: Birthstones, Astrology, anything to do with the New Testament. I had more knowledge about Buddhism and the Bhagavad Gita than I did about the Bible; I began to see the drawbacks to having been raised a mostly secular Jew.

In addition to playing dozens of simulations, watching whatever old recordings of games I could find, and trying to memorize the names and characteristics of assorted gemstones, I worked on my reflexes. At my audition, they'd given me a pen designed to look like a *Jeopardy!* buzzer. I clicked on that pen until my thumb ached and the muscles below it looked like a Virginia ham.

This went on for weeks while I nobly, heroically, didn't smoke pot at all. Finally, it came time to put it all together. After saving three days' worth of *Jeopardy!* episodes in a row on the DVR, I stood behind my big blue leather recliner. I'd intended to die in that chair, but it was obviously dying at a rate faster than me. Nevertheless, it was the only thing in our crappy house that came close to approximating the height of a *Jeopardy!* podium. I held the clicker pen in my right hand. Regina sat off to the side with a notebook. I'd asked her to tally how many questions I missed. Every episode of *Jeopardy!* features sixty questions, plus a Final *Jeopardy!* question. We'd run them all in a row, in real time, including commercials, with no pauses.

When the hour and a half was up, I'd gotten 173 out of 180 questions correct, plus all three Finals.

"I think you're ready," Regina said.

Sober, focused, and totally together for the first time in many years, I exhaled. I'd never been more ready for anything in my life. The next day, Regina and I took our son Elijah out to a swimming hole. It was summer in Central Texas, and that's what you do. This particular swimming hole had a rope swing that flew out over deep water. That's another thing that Texans do in the summer. They pitch themselves into the pool like they're in a Mountain Dew commercial.

Elijah, who was almost eleven—prime rope-swinging age—and I each took a couple of turns, and we were having a great time. The cold water seeped into our bones. It was a perfect summer day. My mind and body felt strong and clear.

"I'm heading back to the rope swing," I said.

"Are you sure?" Regina said.

"Yeah," I said. "I feel great! Elijah, you want to come?"

"My stomach hurts," Elijah said, which is what he always said when he didn't want to do something.

"Maybe we should leave," Regina said.

"Let me just have one more fling," I said.

I climbed up to the tree branch where the rope was tied. The lifeguard handed me the rope. As I launched, my feet slipped. It was a good idea to just drop straight off the rope, feet first, into the water, but on this run, my body went horizontal. I lost my grip. My arms bent back, and my chest smacked into the water, hard. I could feel the tendons tear in my pecs.

I swam to shore. When I got out, my neck and my shoulder were tingling. There was numbness in my right hand. My buzzer hand. It wasn't painful, exactly. But I'd put all my careful calibration and hard work at severe risk because of a dumb impulse that impressed no one. Nothing sums up my life better than that previous sentence.

"I told you not to swing, Dad," Elijah said.

"Dang it," I said.

"You're dumb," he said.

"Maybe," I said. "But I'm still going to be on *Jeopardy!*"

● ● ●

At LAX I hopped off the plane with a dream and my cardigan. A light-blue convertible Beetle awaited me at the rental-car place. I zipped onto the highway, wind blowing through what remained of my hair, like the free-spirited heroine in a quirky late-sixties comedy. Los Angeles, the scene of my greatest failure and most substantial drug use, would soon become a place of sobriety and triumph.

I'd flown as cheaply as possible on Southwest Airlines and had booked a discounted room at a Doubletree as part of a weekly block set aside for *Jeopardy!* and *Wheel of Fortune* contestants. The show paid for nothing, though if you finished third, the worst of all possible fates, you still got $1,000, which more or less covered the cost of your travel.

But I wasn't there to finish third. I'd come to finish first. I was not, to quote the famous lyrics to a musical that hadn't yet been written, "throwing away my shot." This was the trivia Olympics, except I represented no nation other than myself, and no one would be in the stands cheering for me. Except for my mom and dad. They'd made the drive from Phoenix. I was very self-inspired. The music, the moment; I owned it.

My room wasn't ready when I got to the hotel.

"I want a high floor, not facing the highway and far away from the elevators," I requested. Nothing would be left to chance. Nothing would disturb my trivia beauty sleep!

"We'll see what we can do, sir," said the clerk.

"Is there any place I can eat within walking distance?" I asked. Yes, I had a car, but I had no plans to drive around LA seeking temptation. I was entering a Zen-like sequester of the mind. She recommended a fried-chicken place, which sounded delicious but counter-productive.

"There's a Soup Plantation at the mall down the street," she said.

The Soup Plantation! We'd eaten at the one in Pasadena so many times with our toddler back when we'd lived in LA and life hadn't crushed our dreams. Despite its very questionable name, the Soup Plantation is actually an incredible place to eat because you can pile your plates high with unlimited salad and eat unlimited bowls of soup, and there are also cheesy breads and pizzas and a soft-serve frozen yogurt machine and a lemonade dispenser. It's like a collegiate dining hall, but for everyone! In a restaurant world where you sit down on an uncomfortable recycled milk crate and pay $18 for two charred octopus tentacles, the Soup Plantation is the ultimate bargain restaurant, giving the impression of nutrition but actually stuffing you full of cheese calories. It would feed my brain and feed my soul, at a substantial discount. To the Soup Plantation!

By the time I returned from supper, my room was ready, as I requested, on a high floor, not facing the 405, away from the elevators. It was late summer, the sun was still shining, but I drew the blackout shades anyway, turned up the room fan to high, put my phone into airplane mode, turned on the white noise app, put a pillow on the floor, sat on it, crossed my legs, placed my hands on my knees drawn into *tadaka mudra,* the yogic seal of wisdom, and, setting the timer for an hour, entered into the deepest meditation of my life. This room in the Doubletree in West LA would be my *shala* as I meditated on the sacred words: "Holy shit, I am going to be on *Jeopardy!*"

It was 8:00 p.m. I called home briefly. Then I brushed my teeth, took six melatonin capsules, and put myself to bed, dreaming of Trebek's mustache.

At 2:30 a.m., I opened my eyes. The room was silent save for the whoosh of various noise machines and the beating of my hideous heart. I wrenched around in the starchy sheets for a while, but I knew the truth. There would be no more sleep that night, possibly ever again. I opened my laptop to a website called Glo. Despite the horrible name, it was actually a really useful site, containing thousands of yoga and meditation classes from some of the world's leading teachers. For several years I've paid $18 a month—about the cost of one yoga class—and I've gone to it pretty much every day. You can adjust Glo for any purpose. At various times I've used it to build core strength, stretch my hips, try to get my knees to the floor in cobbler's pose, learn about the history of Buddhism, and, more recently, to recover from addiction. In those pre-dawn hours, though, I used it to help my body and my mind get ready for *Jeopardy!*

I clicked on a Yoga Nidra video taught by Jo, an attractive Australian woman whose kind, soothing voice could calm you in any circumstance, even waiting in line to renew your driver's license. Yoga Nidra, which translates to "yogic sleep," is a technique, thousands of years old, which allows the body and mind to enter a deep transcendent meditative state, beyond sleeping or waking, that allows you to briefly touch the highest states of consciousness. At the beginning, Jo asked me to think of a statement. "It is your heart's desire," she said. "It is already true."

"*I am a* Jeopardy! *champion,*" I said to myself over and over again. "*I am a* Jeopardy! *champion. I am a* Jeopardy! *champion.*"

Then she led me through a Yoga Nidra, using a classical script. I imagined myself as very heavy, as very light, as very cold, as very hot. There were visualizations: a mountain, an eagle flying high. I visualized every part of my body relaxing. Veering in and out of my conscious mind, I continually repeated to myself, "*I am a* Jeopardy! *champion*" until I persuaded myself that it was true.

The Yoga Nidra ended.

I looked at the clock.

It was 3:15 a.m. We weren't due at the studio until after nine.

So I did it again. And then a third time. By the time the sun came up, I was fully powered, totally charged up, the readiest game-show contestant in the history of game shows. This was going to be my day.

I suited up, putting on a sport coat and a pressed white dress shirt. Then I ate breakfast and took the shuttle to the Sony studios with my fellow contestants. We made nervous but friendly conversation, as we were soon going to have to destroy one another. We filled out paperwork and went through a full orientation. I drank two cups of heavily leaded coffee. The lead contestant coordinator told us to "play your game." For about half an hour, we practiced on the set, which was vast and impressive. The board loomed over us like the scoreboard at Wrigley. Then it came time to play.

The questions of the day at *Jeopardy!* are drawn randomly by a PricewaterhouseCoopers accountant. So are the names of each contestant, except for the defending champion. I was not in the first grouping, of which the defending champion, a young graduate student from Austin named Jared Hall, made short work. After a short break, they taped the next episode. I wasn't in that group either. Nor was I in the third. By the time we hit lunch, Jared was still standing, now a five-win colossus who'd accumulated more than $150K. Those of us who remained were nervous, facing the prospect of having to play one of the better *Jeopardy!* contestants of all time.

After an uncomfortable lunch in the Sony cafeteria, we returned to the set. I continued sitting in the stands, waiting for my number to be called. If you're curious, no, it's not particularly fun to watch four episodes of *Jeopardy!* in a row on no sleep while wearing a suit. I looked over at my parents, who seemed bored and hungry, as they bore witness to Jared Hall destroy dream after dream. I was not selected for episode four, or episode five, either. Finally, Jared fell. But I was still sitting there, untested.

I went back to the hotel and went back to Soup Plantation. Again, at 8:00 p.m., I drew back the blinds. This time, I snapped awake at 1:00 a.m. The clock said Tuesday. I did my Yoga Nidra again. And again. And again. I was worth something, way more than my detractors (who, at this point, existed only in my mind) said. I wanted to show the world that I could win!

It was the long night of my trivia soul.

● ● ●

I was on *Jeopardy!* at last, and I was going to lose. Not only that, but it looked like I was going to lose epically, disastrously, as badly as Wolf Blitzer had, but even worse, because I wasn't playing for charity. This had the potential to be one of the worst *Jeopardy!* performances of all time. At the end of the first round, one of my opponents had a powerful $8,300. The other had $6,800. I was at $600. You don't have to know anything about *Jeopardy!* to deduce that I was way behind, as I deserved to be.

We went to commercial break. I gazed plaintively into the crowd and saw my mother's face. She looked like she had indigestion. Actually, she always looked at bit like that. But it was a severe case this time. She was in agony. And so was I. All of that preparation—months of clicking the *Jeopardy!* pen they had given me at my audition, rereading Shakespeare, studying the essential facts of botany and geology, learning about birthstones—meant nothing. I'd trained like an elite athlete, and for what? Nothing but humiliation.

The first game of my second day in the stands had again skipped me. By that point, my nerves felt like they'd been shredded through a cheese grater. Nothing could relax my brain now. I was the last person left from my original group, save the current champion, Matt Volk—a tall, financial analyst bro from Cedar Rapids, Iowa, who had won two games, pulling in more than thirty-five grand. I sat alone, slowly going mad.

The contestant coordinator called the name of Loni Geerlings, a freelance editor from Redwood City, California.

She had long curly, blonde hair and a shy smile that the nerd perverts who watch *Jeopardy!* really liked on Twitter when the episode aired a month later. Then he looked at me in the eye and whispered:

"You."

Finally! I went into makeup, saying to the makeup lady, "I'll see you in about thirty minutes for another layer."

"That's what they all say," she said.

I'd randomly drawn the middle podium. Volk stood to my right, Geerlings to my left. I closed my eyes and breathed deep, drawing my hands into *tadaka mudra*. A couple of tech guys walked in front of the contestants.

"For fuck's sake," one of them said, looking at me meditating there on the TV set.

"You like that?" said another.

"No," he said. He'd been living in LA a long time and had enough of these New Age yoga idiots.

The theme music played. Ancient bewigged Johnny Gilbert introduced Alex Trebek, who stepped forward looking sharp and smelling even better. And then the game began and I was living in the dream. My very first *Jeopardy!* category was called "The League Leading Stat." Sports statistics: literally my best subject ever. I was going to leap out to a roaring lead! Unfortunately, I was up against the rarest of *Jeopardy!* things—a smart frat boy who also knew a lot about sports. He had won his title by answering tough questions about the rock band Bad Company and Spike TV's *The Joe Schmo Show*.

Volk ran the first four clues. Finally, on the $1,000 question, I managed to hit the buzzer in time, answering "What is RBI?" to the question "1931: Lou Gehrig, with 184."

I had $1,000 and control of the board. Immediately, I went over to my other specialty topic, literature, a category called "Novel Wives." Unfortunately, Geerlings knew everything about literature as well, plus plenty about science and pop culture. She got the first two questions right. The $600 clue appeared:

"The Many Lives and Secret Sorrows Of Josephine B. ends with Josephine's marriage to him."

I buzzed in.

"Who is Napoleon?" I said, correctly. Now I was cooking with fire. Except that Geerlings rang in ahead of me on the $800 clue about Tolstoy. I've often replayed that in my mind, because the $1,000 clue was the daily double. If I'd gotten the $800 clue, I would have bet all of my $2,400 on the question:

"Z by Therese Anne Fowler is a novel about this real literary wife."

And I would have answered, correctly, "Who is Zelda Fitzgerald?" and I would have had nearly $5,000, and I would have been in great shape.

But Geerlings got it instead. She under-bet severely at $500. I was sitting there at $1,600, where I stayed until the first commercial break; Volk had $2,800 and Geerlings had $1,700.

I didn't get a single question the rest of the first round. Geerlings and Volk outclassed me entirely. Finally, I got in on a category called "Oh, 'G'!" The $1,000 clue was, "Have a heart and name this worldly vegetable seen here"—up popped a photo of an artichoke. I clicked the buzzer and said, "What is an artichoke?"

You may or may not be aware, but *artichoke* doesn't start with *G*.

Geerlings clicked in, said, "What is a GLOBE artichoke?" correctly, and then I was dead. I was getting destroyed.

I didn't want to lose. I'd seen what happens to *Jeopardy!* losers. The day before, as I'd sat in the studio feeling my soul drain into the earth, my fellow contestants were disgorged onto the Sony lot two by two like animals not being allowed onto the ark during the flood, their dreams crushed. The contestant coordinators, who had been so kind all day, said to them, "We called a cab to take you back to the hotel, but you have to pay for it." The entertainment machine was done with them. I wasn't ready for it to be done with me.

But it looked like I didn't have a choice. We went to commercial. Alex Trebek said, "Neal has a lot of catching up to do as we head into *Double Jeopardy!*." I was going down hard.

The makeup lady dusted me, and the sound guy adjusted my mike. Someone raised and lowered the platforms that all of the contestants stand on to make it appear that we were the same height. My hands were shaking, and my brain clouded with a strange fog. I called the main contestant coordinator over. My hand was cramping; I couldn't buzz in time.

"I need a massage!" I cried. She sighed and rubbed my shoulder, performing emotional labor on another weak loser.

The *Jeopardy!* clue board stood in front of me, seemingly forty feet high. Alex came up behind, put his arm around my shoulder and grimaced at the camera. Everyone, win or lose, gets a picture taken with Alex, and that's about the extent of our off-camera interaction. He hid behind a thick veil of inscrutability at all times, presiding over the show with a cruel objectivity like the Old Testament God. That lowered quite a bit in 2019, with the revelation of Alex's stage 4 pancreatic cancer diagnosis. Suddenly, he became much more beloved and avuncular. But when I was on the show, his veil of inscrutability was still very much in place.

Trebek moved on. Another contestant coordinator approached.

"You're having trouble with the buzzer," he said.

"No kidding," I said.

"You're hitting it too hard," he said. "Press it softly. About halfway." I did. "Good," he said. "Now look at me and only me. Listen to my voice. The moment I finish speaking, press the buzzer."

"Okay," I said.

"This is the name of the president who appears on the twenty-dollar bill," he said.

I pressed the buzzer.

"This is the name of the president who appears on the twenty-dollar bill."

Again, I pressed. We did this a half-dozen times.

"That's the rhythm," he said. "That's what you need to do."

The second round started. It got worse. As the guy in third place, I got to choose the first category. I went with "Movie Villains." Volk got the first three right, racking up another $2,000, while doing a decent Dr. Evil imitation in the process, as befitted someone with the confidence of a champion. I cowered and grinned, a sad little man retreating to the shadows.

Geerlings got the $1,600 clue, an easy Jabba the Hutt question that I couldn't ring in for on time, again. Now I trailed by almost ten large, and there were only twenty-seven questions left.

What happened next had little to do with my indefatigable will to win and mostly to do with luck. The $2,000 clue arrived: "The villain in *Galaxy Quest* was named this in dishonor of film critic Andrew." I didn't know the name of the villain in *Galaxy Quest*. But I did know of a much-hated film critic named Andrew. I buzzed in.

"What is Sarris?" I said.

"Yes," said Trebek. "Rhymes with Harris."

Suddenly I had $2,600 to my name.

I moved the board over to "4-Letter U.S. Cities." The $800 clue was "If you've 'bean' watching, you know that on *Glee*, McKinley High is located in this U.S. city."

"What is Lima?" I answered, correctly.

Geerlings got the $1,200 clue: Erie, Pennsylvania. The $1,600 question was "It's located where the Colorado River meets the Gila River in Southwestern Arizona." I hadn't spent all those childhood years in Arizona for nothing, dammit! "What is Yuma?" I answered, and then I had $5K. I picked the $2000 clue.

The answer was . . . the Daily Double.

"You've moved up handsomely," Alex, himself still very handsome well into his seventies, said to me.

I had to choose my wager. But I had no choice. I was still way behind.

"Let's make it a true Daily Double, Alex," I said.

I really said it! On national TV! And the crowd gasped.

The question read, simply: "It's the biggest city on the Big Island."

But the answer didn't come to me immediately. "What is Oahu?" I said to myself, but I knew that wasn't right, because Oahu isn't a Hawaiian city. I thought "Maui" and then "Hana" but saying either of those would have been my doom. I took a breath.

"What is Hilo?" I said.

"That is correct," Trebek said.

I was up to ten grand. From there, in "World War II: On the Home Front," I got $1,200 for answering "What is Nevada?" off "A 1942 Supreme Court decision involving divorces granted in this state made a divorce valid in any state valid in all." I also answered a couple of easy low-money questions in "Heavenly Language" and correctly identified "Vulcan" from the clue "Spock would be proud! This suggestion won a 2013 online poll to name a moon of Pluto." That was another $1,200. Finally, I answered "What is ice fishing?" under the nightmarish category of Types of Fishing for $400. And that was it.

The final buzzer sounded, mercifully leaving two hidden clues in "Types of Fishing." I had $14,000. Volk had $12,800. Geerlings was at $12,000. This one would be close.

The *Final Jeopardy!* category appeared: "Newspapers."

When I was sixteen years old, I was a teen correspondent for the *Phoenix Gazette*. I attended high-school newspaper conventions, and then I graduated from the Medill School of Journalism at Northwestern University. Then I worked as a newspaper reporter, full-time, for eight years. Since then, my freelance writing had appeared in lots of newspapers, including the *New York Times* and the *Wall Street Journal*.

I was going to win *Jeopardy!*.

And I did, because I knew the answer to the clue: "On July 23, 2013, this best-selling British tabloid respelled its name on its masthead to honor big British news."

I wrote down "What is *The Sun*?" So, as it turns out did Geerlings. She bet everything and finished with $24,000. What a great player. So did Volk. He had $25,000. Another great player. But I, in the end, had $26,000. I pumped my fist and raised my arms to the sky. I danced around behind the podium. The spotlight was mine!

My mom slipped away from the stands. She wasn't supposed to, but she did, saying that she had to go to the bathroom. She texted my wife Regina.

"Neal just won *Jeopardy!*," she said.

"How much?" Regina texted back.

"$26,000," she said.

Back in Austin, my wife and son were jumping around our crummy little house, screaming. I was in the green room. I had less than fifteen minutes to change my shirt, take a piss, and get my pancake touched up.

"Man," one of the contestant coordinators said to me, "I thought you were going down in flames."

"No such luck," I said. "I'm the motherfucking *Jeopardy!* champion!"

I may have been flippant and obscene in the dressing room, but I was also genuinely thrilled, and maybe even a little humbled. While I may have accomplished things in my life, I'd never done it on TV. And I'd gleamed out brightly, center stage. Other than the birth of my son, this was the greatest moment of my life. All eyes on me.

Winning *Jeopardy!* was the most fulfilling experience of my life, the ultimate realization and validation of all my dreams. It was also like taking the LSATs at my bar mitzvah while on acid—a brief, distorted gaze into a nightmarish dystopian future where the few remaining educated North Americans are forced to battle one another intellectually, on television, for what amounts to a petty amount of money for all but the biggest winners. *Jeopardy!* is a beloved family institution that also happens to resemble a sinister melding of *The Running Man* and *The Hunger Games,* presided over by a grumpy, cologne-slathered Canadian warlord.

As I'd headed backstage, I'd peeked up into the stands. My father caught my glance. Never one to praise me for anything, he gritted his lips and gave me a little fist pump.

Dad was proud. Mom was proud. I was proud of myself. At a low point in my life, when it seemed like I could never pull myself back into success, I achieved something difficult, against at least moderate odds. And I did it with a crazy comeback.

I was the motherfucking *Jeopardy!* champion.

I just had to do it again.

● ● ●

Game Two was no easier. "Quite often," Alex Trebek said after he came out, "bright people, intelligent people, seem to be more reserved when expressing their emotions. But that wasn't the case on our program yesterday for our new champion Neal Pollack. He was excited, he was happy, and he showed it! And we love that." So very briefly, I'd won Trebek's heart. Now I was up against Kamal Foreman, a very smart Atlanta-area attorney, and Eric Winschel, a roofing contractor from Pasadena. Once again, I limped along in the first round, but not making any fatal errors. I had $3,000, versus Foreman's $3,800 and Winschel's $7,000. It was a deep enough hole, though, that I had to take aggressive action.

"Remember our champion Neal started off slowly on yesterday's program," Trebek handily reminded me. For our second question board, a category called "Authors on Authors" appeared. I had first pick, and immediately dove toward the $2,000 clue. The Daily Double appeared.

"Let's bet it all, Alex," I said.

I was rewarded with this: "Vachel Lindsay's poem 'The Raft' said this author 'in white stands gleaming like a pillar of the night.'" I didn't read the quote very carefully, and only saw the word *raft*, so I trumpeted:

"Who is Thor Heyerdahl?"

"No, it was Mark Twain."

I thudded the podium.

"Start building again," he said.

A "Hemingway," a "Joseph Conrad," a "Kipling," and a *"Planet of the Apes"* later, I came upon "Movie-ending Lines of the Decade" for $2,000. I had regained my total up to $4,400. I bet $4,000:

"All right," Trebek said. "1950s. I now pronounce you men and wives."

"What is *Some Like It Hot*?" I guessed.

But the answer was, in fact, *Seven Brides for Seven Brothers,* and I was down to $400, *way* behind, and, as Trebek reminded me, "There are no more Daily Doubles left to cause you grief."

"Good lord," I said, and began my long march back.

By the end of the round, Foreman had me pinned, but somehow I got the last four questions correct. I had $11,600. But then the judges took $1,600 away from me at the commercial break, because they determined I said "fatigued" instead of "fatigue" for "Starts with an Antonym of," a category so complicated it's not even worth explaining. So heading into

Final Jeopardy!, I had $10,000. Winschel was close behind with $9,400, and Foreman was far ahead of me with $15,200.

The question was: "Since his death in 1989, he's been inducted into the U.S. Hockey, World Figure Skating, and National Inventors Hall of Fame."

I thought I knew the answer immediately, not because I know much about hockey, figure skating, or inventors, but because I'd studied. This answer had come up again and again on *Jeopardy!.* It was part of the show's universe of tricks, like a crossword clue that comes to you if you do enough puzzles.

"Who is Zamboni?" I wrote. I was right. The other two contestants whiffed. And I had won, this time bringing in $19,999. "He's happy once again, and he should be," Alex said, as I pumped my fists. Another miracle. Hell yes!

We had a lunch break at the Sony commissary, giving me an extra hour and a half as *Jeopardy!* champion. I ate a sensible spinach salad with egg and a bowl of chicken soup, sitting there in a very good mood, surrounded by the other contestants from my pool who hadn't yet gotten a chance. We regarded one another awkwardly, because by the end of the day we knew all but one of us would be *Jeopardy!* dead. The contestant coordinators kept us under very tight watch, sequestered more rigidly than a murder jury. It was a glorious hour. We talked about our favorite TV shows.

Then after lunch, I won again, pulling in another fourteen grand-plus on the strength of my knowledge about military academies and Oscar-winning screenplays and despite blowing an easy *Final Jeopardy!* question about the web browser Firefox. Now I was a three-day cash winner, with a total of more than $60,000, and was technically eligible for the Tournament of Champions, the grail for all *Jeopardy!* players. One more win, and I had basically clinched a spot.

By the end of the day, the green room, which had been so full of hope at 8:00 a.m., now felt like a corpse-strewn battlefield. The fruit plate had shriveled, the coffeepots drained. Someone—not me—dropped a huge deuce in one of the toilets. The place stank like the sewers of Paris. If I survived game four, they'd have to fly me back to LA on Monday, this time on the show's nickel, and the whole process would start anew.

But you're not really a *Jeopardy!* player until you experience the one thing nearly every contestant who's ever appeared on the show has in common: losing. Like in vampire lore, they call the person who defeats you in *Jeopardy!* your "maker." Actually, I'm the only one who calls it that, but it feels appropriate, because the person who beats you is the one who teaches you the true meaning of trivia death. They bear an awesome responsibility to carry you through to the other side. I'd been the maker for six unfortunate souls. And though I didn't know it yet, I'd already met my maker.

At lunch, I bit into an olive pit. The inside of my mouth felt a little tender. Maybe, I thought, I'd chipped a tooth.

"Does my mouth look weird to you?" I said to the young woman sitting next to me, opening wide.

She peered in.

"You're fine, Neal," she said.

Sarah Zucker was not about to be intimidated by my freewheeling hipster idiot act. She was also Jewish, she'd attended the same college as me, and she was an avant-garde video artist and scriptwriter from Los Angeles. Any aspirations to cool I had, she had more. Within two hours, she was going to beat me. Barely.

We were playing against an options trader from Chicago named Andrew, who was also a solid contestant. But I had the buzzer advantage, and the experience. I sprinted out to a huge early lead but dropped $3,000 on a Daily Double when I answered the Red Cross instead of the March Of Dimes. Then there was a category called "Space Shuttle Flyovers," and they showed the Shuttle flying over Dodger Stadium. I rang in.

"What is Dodger Stadium?" I said.

"That is cor—" Trebek said.

"Home of the World Champion Dodgers!" I added.

The Dodgers were not World Champions then. And, as of this writing, they are still not. That was lame in every single way. Then after the commercial break, we had to do our contestant's chatter. I'd just about run out of things to talk about with Trebek, so I blathered on about how my son was into the very lucrative world of competitive video games.

"You can win a lot of money!" I said.

"More than in this game?" he said.

"We'll see!" I said.

"Yes," Trebek said ominously. "We'll see . . ."

If he'd had the power to pull a lever and drop me through the floor right there, he would have. Regardless, the final curse had been placed upon my soul. In Round Two, I said Hamlet when I should have said King Lear, which meant I lost control of the Shakespeare category and also meant that Zucker got to boost her score big-time by identifying an easy quote from Lady MacBeth. From there, it was back and forth the whole way. I screwed up when I didn't buzz in even though I completely knew that guy in the photo was Dwight Yoakam. And then, for the very final question of the round, Zucker got a Daily Double in a category about bears. She knew the answer, and she was ahead.

Final Jeopardy! was "European Geography," and this clue:

"Since a national split in 1993, it's the only world capital that borders two other countries—Austria and Hungary."

Well, shit, I didn't know that! I guessed Prague, which Trebek said was "close, but no cigar." The correct answer was Bratislava. Andrew missed it and lost all his money. Zucker missed it and only had $1799. I'd had $12,600. I lost all but $1 of it. Unlike in the other games, where I'd been way behind and had come back and won with a Hail Mary, here I'd been way ahead and had gone down hard, with a huge, stupid bet. And it was over.

Was that really it? A half hour later, I staggered out into the blinding LA August sunlight, and realized that no one on the Sony lot knew that I'd been on *Jeopardy!,* and no one cared. In reality, I hadn't played all that well, but I'd been gritty and bold and had earned $62,798, probably about half of what Trebek had earned that day. I felt buzzy, numb, and weird as I put on my sunglasses.

My parents approached.

"We're very hungry," my mother said. "Your father's blood sugar is dropping. We have to get something to eat . . . now."

Back to reality. It would be weeks before I gathered all my friends in a Mexican restaurant in Austin at 4:30 p.m. on a Tuesday, so they could all watch me almost lose and then spectacularly win. When it aired, I got to relive the glory all over again. Then there were toasts. Then there was tequila. But immediately after my greatest triumph, my parents and I went to a hipster burger joint where my mother said, "The meat is a little underdone." They didn't raise a toast to me, they just stared at me blankly while I gave a boring rehash of the game-show events they'd just witnessed.

"I'm glad you didn't win again," Mom said. "Enough of that nonsense."

Ah, dear mother. Always striking the right balance between supportive and dismissive. I think she just wanted it to be over because watching me walk that tightrope stressed her out too much. How I miss her.

As soon as my parents dropped me off at home, I called Regina and talked excitedly at her for an hour. I'd won enough money so that we could maybe put a down payment on a house, and also maybe take a trip. I had done it; through the miracle of television, I'd clawed us back into the middle class.

"I'm proud of you," she said.

"I'm proud of me, too," I said.

Then I got into the Beetle and drove to Jerod and Joanne's house.

"You're not going to believe what just happened to me," I said.

Jerod handed me a lit joint. I took a huge drag. At last, I could be reunited with my one true love, marijuana. I got super-high and forgot all about trivia.

Much later, back in my hotel, I stuffed a towel under the door and smoked a fatty while taking a huge, well-earned dump. I clicked onto YouTube, where I watched the final scene of *Rocky II* over and over again. My eyes filled with tears as I got high on the toilet.

"I did it," I blubbered, baked out of my wits. "I did it."

Man, I was a real winner.

THE WEIRD TURN PRO

I loved marijuana. Loved loved loved loved it. I loved it so much that I wanted to marry it. The fact that I was already married didn't matter. Maybe I could be married to Regina *and* to marijuana. They could be sister wives! Sure, Regina provided support and guidance and understanding. Marijuana, on the other hand, made watching *Thor: The Dark World* fun. Regina had enjoyed watching that movie too. But she did it sober, which was totally weak.

When Regina and I decided to get married, we pledged to always support each other's artistic ambitions. She would back my writing and I would stand behind her calling to paint, and over the years, we'd held that line. I'd published ten books and she kept painting, working as a professor at a community college and making better and better work, never earning a lot of money but still doing gallery shows. We'd kept our modest dream alive.

In 2014, mostly thanks to my *Jeopardy!* winnings, we moved into a three-bedroom, two-bath 1980s ranch house in near-suburban Austin. Regina converted our two-car garage into a painting studio and I had one bedroom as an office. Elijah, now twelve years old, had the second bedroom, and Regina and I slept in the master with our little old Boston terrier, Hercules. There we were, Regina and I, married fourteen years, living with our little family and a lot of marijuana.

"Maybe you should cut back on the weed a little," Regina said.

"Maybe I should cut back on *you*," I said.

She didn't like that much.

Cut back on marijuana: how absurd! Why would I do that? Marijuana wasn't alcohol, or cocaine or sugar. Decades of propaganda had labeled it a drug, but I knew that wasn't true. In fact, I argued, marijuana was actually a *health food*, green like kale and ten times more stimulating than tea. It didn't just provide a little chill while listening to music. Marijuana formed the foundation of my existence, a vapeable vitamin as vital to my daily routine as all the interesting things I did while I was high. It was *healing* people all over the world. With the help of marijuana, I would live forever, and I would be amazing.

I thought about marijuana constantly: where to consume it, how to buy it, how to mooch it, and all the enthralling experiences I would and did have under its influence. I constantly advocated for it and tried to get other people to do it with me. When people told me that marijuana "just didn't do anything" for them, I said, almost rudely, "You just haven't found your strain yet."

As far as I was concerned, *everyone* needed to be high, all the time, except for maybe firefighters in the middle of their shift. But I didn't have a problem, no ma'am. I had the *solution*.

It was marijuana.

Soon, I came up with the perfect way to get as much marijuana as I possibly could without paying for all of it:

"I'm going to become a marijuana journalist," I said to my wife.

"Of course you are," she said.

It would be the perfect job for me. So I knew how to interview people and craft pitches and not plagiarize and not get sued. I could simultaneously be a journalist *and* consume lots of THC.

"I'm a real professional," I said to Regina. "It's perfect. This is the golden age of liberty!"

"Great," she said, rolling her eyes.

"You don't understand," I said. "It's like if coffee had been illegal your whole life, and you loved coffee, but it was hard to get and it wasn't always the best quality. But then suddenly coffee became legal and it was the most amazing coffee you could imagine. That's what this is like!"

"Except that it's not coffee," she said. "It's marijuana."

"Better than coffee!" I said.

The legal states had even started serving marijuana-*infused* coffee. Maybe I'd even do a story about that. I wanted to cover whatever could get me high.

Regina couldn't criticize me this time, because I was going to get paid! To smoke weed! My plan was foolproof, which was good. Because I was definitely being a fool.

A guy I knew named Ricardo Baca became the editor of *The Cannabist,* an online marijuana newspaper published by the *Denver Post.* It was the first time a mainstream news organization had covered cannabis in this way, and he was the first official "marijuana journalist" in America. I wanted some of whatever he was ingesting. He came to Austin for South by Southwest because he was the star of *Rolling Papers,* a documentary about pot journalism.

I wanted to be in a documentary about pot journalism. Maybe I could star in the sequel, or maybe I could be the star of a Vice TV show about a similar subject. I would be hilarious in that role. It was a plan. Quickly, and by design, I turned a minor professional acquaintance into a close and trusted ally. The age of legal marijuana was coming—maybe not in Texas, but in a lot of other places. I had to get in on the action. As a writer, which, as always, involved the least amount of work possible.

○ • •

The *New York Times* profiled an online marijuana ad agency called Cannabrand whose founders said they were "weeding out the stoners" and that dispensaries looked like "underground abortion clinics." I responded with my first *Cannabist* editorial, a pretentious and angry piece titled, "Don't Let Pot Be Just Another Yuppie Lifestyle Accoutrement."

I wrote that when I read the *Times* article, "I got pissed, because I am a stoner. And I was especially pissed because I was traveling on business and couldn't do what I usually do when I get pissed, which is smoke weed. Or vape it. Or eat a candy." In other words, I was without my yuppie lifestyle accoutrement. I continued:

> Here's the thing about stoners: Some of them are CEOs and moms. They are also, occasionally, shiftless losers. And self-employed entrepreneurs and small business owners. And doctors. And musicians. And comedians. And professional athletes. And novelists. And lawyers. And scientists. And movie stars. And cops. I've smoked with all those types of people in my life. I've smoked with most of those types of people this year.

That sounds like the writing of someone who likes marijuana a little too much. I was saying that *anyone* can be a drug addict! But I didn't see it that way. The mid-2010s revolution was coming, and I was going to storm the Winter Palace.

"We need to figure out how to get me a job covering this beat," I wrote in an email to Ricardo.

He offered to introduce me to some people at *High Times*. But I didn't want to write for *High Times*. I wanted to be part of the brave new world of legitimate marijuana journalism. It was going to happen, no doubt.

A couple weeks later, Ricardo called me while I was getting high behind a ramen shop in North Austin.

"Hey, man," he said. "I've been thinking. I was wondering if you'd be interested in being the Texas correspondent for *The Cannabist*."

"Aw, fuck yeah!" I said.

This would be, he explained, an extremely part-time gig. They could give me $400 an article, which made me *The Cannabist*'s top freelancer. Considering Ricardo assigned me, at most, one article a month, this didn't really make for a sustainable living. But I didn't care.

As a marijuana journalist on the beat, I should have cared about a lot of things: the politics of weed, the science behind growing weed, the economics of the booming marijuana business, social justice, racial justice, weed-related gentrification, and many other topics. Maybe I cared about the politics, a little, if only because it was so difficult to get Texas politicians interested in legalization. But in reality, becoming a marijuana journalist meant one thing to me, and one thing only. I was going to get really high all the time. Which I did already. But now I was going to earn a part-time salary to do it.

GANJA YOGA

I was into yoga almost as much as I was into marijuana. Nearly every day, I'd unfurl my mat, either at home or in some room somewhere in town, and grind myself through an hour or more (or less) of poses, breath exercises, and meditation. It was my church, my social life, and the moral anchor of my life. And I pretty much always did it high.

I'd been practicing yoga for a decade. Regina advised me to start when I had a meltdown after the *New York Times* gave *Never Mind the Pollacks* a bad review. And I loved it; yoga made my body feel great and my mind feel calm. And I loved doing it stoned.

A few years after I started practicing, Richard Freeman, one of America's wisest and most experienced yoga teachers, accepted me into his Ashtanga yoga teacher training. My co-trainees included yoga studio owners and people who had been practicing much longer, and in a more rigorous way, than I had, but Richard told me he accepted me because "I thought you'd enjoy it."

Richard warned us against the dangers of getting high. He had authority to do this because he lives in Boulder, Colorado, where marijuana is in everything, including, probably, the water supply. People had been coming to his classes stoned since the Nixon Administration.

Be careful of marijuana, Richard said. Smoking it often leads to ecstatic states, even a feeling of transcendence. But it's short-lived and ephemeral, and it has a dark side. Yoga, on the other hand, can provide a permanent state of well-being and calm. Richard offered no shortcuts to *samadhi*, the state of intense concentration and inner peace that represents the final stage of yoga achievement. You just had to practice with full diligence and allow it to come gradually. Don't mistake getting high for that feeling, he said. He said that although marijuana may allow you to experience ecstatic yoga states "temporarily within a limited field," the overall effect is that the mind is less able to focus.

But what the hell did Richard know? He only drank wine on ceremonial occasions and hadn't done drugs in nearly forty years! I often transcended things when I was high, such as the ability to understand the plotlines of the movies and TV shows that I was watching. I felt like I was floating above my body all the time.

I made many wonderful friends while I was in Boulder, including a young woman who lived near the training center with her fiancé. In those pre-legalization years, they had a little side business selling weed. On lunch break or after class, we'd go over to their townhouse near the studio where they kept jars and jars of the stickiest shit imaginable. Some days I'd just sit there in my little sleeveless yoga shirt and gaze at the crystal buds with wonder. Other times, I'd inhale the deep purple or sharp tangerine odor, entranced by the erotic and magical power of home-grown Colorado terpenes.

On the best days, I'd hork a bong hit and feel my ass sink into the couch in a state of *samadhi*-plus.

That usually happened on the weekends, though. One afternoon I went to class high as balls. Oftentimes we spent the afternoon sessions in boring anatomy lectures or giving each other adjustments, stuff in which I had scant interest. However, on this day, Richard seemed annoyed with us for having been lazy and too chatty in our practices. He ran us through a series of intense and very difficult arm balances. My head hurt. I was high, this was supposed to be fun. Did he know? He knew. He had to. Either way, I was miserable, so I got high again after class.

I did everything high, but I especially did yoga high. Because marijuana made everything better, and because yoga was the best thing, the two together became the *super-best thing*. They were a transcendence combo pack, like the sausage-and-cheese samplers at Buc-ee's, which is a super rest-stop chain found on Texas highways. I got high before my volunteer sessions at the neighborhood yoga studio, before practicing at home, before practicing in public, and often even before teaching. Sometimes I thought the weed improved my focus, and sometimes it would distract me. But it didn't matter. I floated along blissfully, or so I thought.

When my family moved back to Austin in the summer of 2011, I quickly fell in with a group of friends. We did yoga together every Sunday morning; we called ourselves the Yoga Pals. Part of being a Yoga Pal meant meeting up before class at a house near our studio, where we all got high. We all brought our own pipes and our own supply. I'd leave my house around 9:00 a.m. in my sandals and my exercise shorts. My yoga mat bag held a sweat towel, the mat itself, a lighter, a little glass pipe, and a grinder with some weed in it. For a while it was a grinder that looked like a poker chip. When I misplaced that one while I was stoned, I got one for my birthday with Willie Nelson's name on it.

The Yoga Pals baked up and then we went to do yoga. When yoga ended, most days we'd go back to the house, glistening with sweat and relaxation, for a little mini-bong session. Sometimes brunch followed. I'd drive home blasted out of my mind, listening to a vintage reggae show on community-supported radio. And then when I got home, I got high again.

It was a lifestyle, and not a bad one, either. But it had its limits. Yoga promises relaxation, but you're also supposed to connect more deeply with the world around you. I rarely connected with anything besides how good I felt. Like a dog who goes nuts when you open the refrigerator, I didn't care about anything beyond what I could get down my gullet.

During those early days of legalization, I realized I wasn't alone. Yoga stoner was an actual genre of person—my type of person. As a marijuana journalist, I was duty-bound to investigate this important phenomenon.

● ● ●

One night in early 2015, an Uber dropped me in front of a building on one of the darker blocks just south of downtown San Francisco. I may have been *The Cannabist*'s Texas correspondent, but there was only so much weed news out of Texas, and that news was usually "Nope, still not legal yet." It was a Monday night in March 2015. I'd traveled more than a thousand miles so I could get stoned during a yoga class. This was the place where that happened. I looked up at the hand-painted sign.

"Merchants of Reality," it read.

The door to the building was open, with a locked metal gate in front. I rang the buzzer. A young man came down the stairs. Handsome and bearded and wearing flannel, he leaned in toward the gate.

"Are you here for the gathering?" he said.

"Sure!" I said.

I walked up the stairs. The walls were covered in interesting collage. At the top was some sort of papier-mâché art that looked like a flowery octopus. I'd fallen down the rabbit hole.

According to my host, Merchants of Reality's building originally had been a hotel in 1906. It had been through many incarnations since, but it was now a nonprofit art space where some dudes lived. In those last fertile days before full legalization came to California, it was also a licensed medical-marijuana cooperative. They grew their own. And if you had an MMJ card in California, you could legally smoke weed on the premises. You could even smoke weed while doing yoga.

I'd heard that a yoga teacher in San Francisco was offering several "Ganja Yoga" classes a week, where students actually smoked on their mats during practice. I cashed in some frequent flier miles and flew there as soon as I could to check it out. For years, I'd dreamed of this reality. If a teacher tried a stunt like that in Texas, they'd be looking at twenty years in Huntsville.

I couldn't wait to be among my people.

The Ganja Yoga class was supposed to start at 7:15. It was 7:10, and I was the only person who'd showed up.

"Do you have your MMJ card?" he asked.

"No, man," I said. "I'm from Texas. I have nothing."

He told me I could go on the balcony to smoke a joint. That wasn't technically on the property, he said, so it was my problem if I got caught. It seemed like the balcony was on the property to me, but I wanted to get high, so I didn't argue. As to how I'd obtained the weed, I was in California. It wasn't hard.

While I stood outside, barefoot, in fifty-degree weather, the teacher, Dee Dussault, arrived, a Canadian hippie bearing too many candles and dozens of little sample bags of THC-infused pretzels made by a startup company, which she'd been given to share with her students. She apologized that no one else had come to the class. Predicting such things can be difficult for any yoga teacher.

"I don't know," she said, handing me a bag of weed pretzels for free. "Maybe people just don't want to do Ganja Yoga on a Monday."

But people did, as it turned out. They were just stoners, so they were late. As they arrived, Dussault checked them in; if they hadn't been to class before, they had to join the cooperative so they could get stoned in the yoga room.

By 7:45, three other students had arrived: an attractive female yoga teacher from the East Bay, a massive bodybuilder who, as I smoked out with him on the balcony, gave an excoriating speech against George Will, and a regular-looking middle-aged guy wearing a black hoodie.

Dussault liked to start Ganja Yoga by sitting in a candle-lit circle where the students introduce themselves and explain why they've come to class. The East Bay yoga teacher said she'd been getting high and doing yoga by herself for a while and wanted to see what it was like in public. The bodybuilder said, unsurprisingly, that he needed to work on his body. The hoodie guy said, "Hi, I'm John. I like pot. I hurt my back last week. I saw this class online. And I thought it might help."

Two minutes later, I sat on my borrowed yoga mat, stoned out of my wits, my hands devotionally in the air above my head. Dussault said, "Let's all give gratitude to cannabis. Plant medicine." Life was but a dream.

Whatever weed I had smoked—and I had smoked several varieties—was very strong, and I'd had a couple of those special pretzels, too. This wasn't like taking a little puff of Mexican ditch garbage before grinding through my daily yoga hour at home.

We moved languidly through some mellow poses, stretching out our shoulders and our hips, mindfully watching our breath, our gazes softly focused, sometimes closing our eyes. After nearly ten hours of consecutive travel, it felt incredible. My joints relaxed; my bones realigned. The connective fascia of my lower back broadened and unraveled. My hip flexors lengthened. The physical and mental stress of my long travel day, all my quotidian worries and neuroses, dissipated into nothingness. I had full awareness of my body rearranging itself at a cellular level.

We lay in *savasana*, final resting pose, otherwise known as "corpse pose." It had never felt so pleasant to be a corpse.

"And now it's intermission," Dussault said.

"Intermission?" I said.

"So people can go to the bathroom or put on socks or chat," she said.

"Oh," I said.

"But mostly so they can get high."

These classes, as far as I could tell, were about 90 percent yoga and 10 percent ganja. People were welcome to smoke during the classes, Dussault told me, but they mostly did it before class and at intermission.

For now, though, it was break time, and we all got high out on the balcony, chatting like old friends. "It's like in college," said the bodybuilder. "You find out who's got the weed, and then you go, 'Heeeeeeey!'"

We went back inside and lay down.

Dussault confidently led us through a guided meditation, which included a lovely color-coded tour through our body's chakra system, yogic energy centers that correspond with moods or states of being. She ended with the *sahasrara*, the crown chakra, having us imagine a great beam of light shooting from the tops of our heads. That wasn't hard to do. I was so high. Or was I? The difference wasn't exactly clear.

A chill breeze flowed through the almost-dirty room. My yoga mat smelled like eight different shades of ass. Outside, there was a lot of traffic noise. Inside, I could hear people doing dishes. It didn't matter. My body glowed with ecstasy.

As I arched my back, I felt my thoughts and sensations becoming one with the infinite universe.

I'd been in San Francisco for two hours.

When class ended, my Uber driver picked me up, and suddenly the non-ecstatic aspects of being stoned began to set in. I hadn't eaten anything but THC-infused pretzels in ten hours.

"Dude I am *starving*," I said to the driver. "Is there somewhere I can get a pizza?"

"Like a slice?" he asked.

"No, man," I said. "A *whole* pizza."

He did know of a place. I called ahead. He stopped there, meter running, while I waited. Then he took me to where I was staying, basically a door in a wall in an alley between two unremarkable commercial buildings.

"Have you been here before?" he said, worried.

"Naw, it's all good," I said. "I'm high and I just did yoga."

"If you say so," he said, and drove away.

For ten minutes, I stood in the alley fumbling with a lock box while my dinner iced over. Finally I stumbled into my apartment, which was gray and dingy and low-ceilinged. It looked like the residence of a character who was about to be murdered in a Raymond Chandler novel.

I sat at the kitchen table, surrounded by nothing, and scarfed a whole cold pizza in about two minutes. The Buddha himself had never achieved such transcendence.

● ● ●

On the website of his Boulder-based studio, The Yoga Workshop, my guru Richard Freeman wrote,

> When relationships, details of everyday life and one's own yoga practice are dealt with under the influence of marijuana, the result is often a lack of completion, an absence of external feedback and an inability to postpone pleasure. Yoga practitioners who smoke

during, or after their practice on a regular basis tend to plateau in their practice and gradually lose their edge, their intellectual capacity and brilliance. They lose the ability to watch their minds on deep levels and wind up grasping for pleasurable states without having completed the work and understanding that would normally give rise to such states.

That was not what I wanted to hear. I preferred Dussault's philosophy. She also taught naked yoga and worked as a sex and relationships counselor. Plus, unlike Richard Freeman, she didn't make me read the Upanishads as homework. She told me,

"I think cannabis and yoga are so powerful when combined because both already lend themselves to becoming more embodied, sensually-aware, relaxed, and receptive to 'non-ordinary states' of consciousness. Sensually, both yoga and cannabis encourage the user to really go deep into things like how music feels in one's body, or to notice the way the sunlight shines on the lake just so. They both can help us become more present to the world around and inside us, to temporarily, but increasingly, move beyond the linear, goal-oriented, conditioned experiences that tend to comprise much of daily life in our frenzied, busy, competitive era."

These were the two perspectives competing for my attention. The ganja won, as it usually did.

The next night, I got stoned in Golden Gate Park, and then went to a place on Haight Street called The Red Victorian, an "experimental hotel" run by a "culture-hacking collective" that offered classes in building permaculture gardens, indigenous solidarity, and "experimental dinners where *you* are the experiment." The Embassy Suites, it was not. Dussault led me and about twenty other people through a yoga class while Thai massage therapists worked us over with cannabis-based muscle balm. "Feel the cannabis working with your body,"

Dussault said, along with "feel like you're moving through maple syrup," a Canadianism rarely heard in a US yoga class.

The next night, a Wednesday, I returned to Merchants of Reality for my third consecutive day of Ganja Yoga. My neighbors and I lolled about pleasantly, sharing pipes and joints, chewing on little candies. Then a chipper-looking young woman bounced up off her mat and announced she worked for a marijuana delivery service.

"I have lollipops!" she said. "Grape, fudge-flavored, cherry, and, my favorite, cinnamon! You guys, they are great! They are so awesome!"

We bum-rushed her like kids who'd just seen the ice-cream truck.

After she was done handing out candy, the woman took a photo of her assistant smoking a bowl on her mat and posted it on Instagram. Dussault later told me that this person wasn't the official sponsor, that people had just been coming to class, making announcements, and passing out drugs like uninvited pharma reps.

The official sponsor, a nervous-looking woman with long blonde pigtails hanging out from a spangled pink bicycle helmet, wandered in a few minutes later to set up a display table of free, potent marijuana samples. She explained that she was the founder of the "first farm-to-table medical marijuana delivery service," which came with an app for users to review the soil content of their artisanal weed. When you ordered your cannabis, she delivered it to your house via bicycle.

What the fuck is going on? I thought, and not just because I was stoned.

The sponsor dashed away to make her deliveries, and we all calmly sat in a circle. Dussault instructed us to cross our legs and close our eyes, then she passed around a joint of OG Ogre Kush, left by the bicycle lady.

The woman to my right tapped my knee and passed the joint over. I took a long, deep inhale and coughed violently.

I could barely breathe as I headed to the mat. For the first twenty minutes, I staggered. The OG Ogre was some strong shit. I felt kind of nauseous, and more than a little confused. Clearly, I had overmedicated.

When I wrote an article about this strange experience for *The Cannabist*, I claimed that I'd used my extreme yoga powers to overcome getting too high, that I "gently and bemusedly observed the situation." As usual, I'd seen what I'd wanted to see. "I had a choice," I wrote. "I could let the cannabis control me, or I could control the cannabis. Yoga takes priority over all things in my life. It is the boss, not the weed."

But I was lying to myself.

Weed was the boss.

A few years later, when I was about eighteen months clean, I got an email from Dussault celebrating the ten-year anniversary of Ganja Yoga. She'd written a book, was working on releasing forty online classes, and had certified Ganja Yoga teachers in Calgary, Denver, Tulsa, Seattle, New Hampshire, and Hawaii, among others. She asked me to write about her anniversary tour, where she'd be giving pot-yoga teacher trainings in Toronto, LA, New York City, Montreal, Detroit, and Oakland.

My email response: "I am still writing, but I also realized that I'm a marijuana addict so I'm not writing about marijuana anymore (unless it relates to addiction). It just wasn't serving my purposes anymore. But I am happy for your success and wish you luck!"

She wrote back suggesting that I should try CBD oil. Or at least chocolate or mango. "Stay young and healthy, Neal!" she said.

"Yoga never hurts," I wrote back.

She responded, ":)."

THE BAKLAVA
OF DEATH

It was the summer of 2015 and weed was busting out all over. Oregon legalized it, and I needed to get there fast so I could get high. Fortunately, I got assigned a car junket in Portland. It was nothing special as car junkets go. I was testing the new Smart ForTwo, a tiny car that would soon be obsolete. In addition to writing about myself and about weed, I also traveled around the world on luxury junkets, driving the finest vehicles and vomiting around some of the most glamorous racetracks in the world. I drove a Rolls Royce in the hills above Cannes, a different Rolls Royce down the coast of South Africa, an electric Jaguar across the Corinth canal, a Subaru through a canyon on Oahu, and countless other cars on countless other world highways. I flew first-class to Europe dozens of times.

One night I stayed in a Frank Gehry-designed hotel in the wine country of Andalusia and had a four-room suite with its own private vineyard. There's a reason you never see a negative car review; this is how auto journalists live.

And I didn't even like cars. I thought they were kind of stupid, except for the electric ones. If this makes me sound lucky, then yes, I'm, really, really lucky. But I was still willing to piss it all away on weed.

The marijuana news was dead in Texas, so I had to earn my marijuana journalism stripes somehow. I connived to spend a couple extra days on official *Cannabist* business.

"Dude," I said to my editor, "this is the story of the year. Freedom is rising."

He agreed to pay me just enough to cover most of my expenses. The car company handled the plane ticket, and I weaseled my way into staying with my friends Michael and Kristina. Like all good addicts, I placed the substance at the top of the list and did everything I could to gain total access.

When I arrived in late August, Oregon had technically legalized, but marijuana wasn't on sale in stores yet. My somewhat dubious thesis was that I would report on the "endless possibility" of freedom as the state revved up for its on-sale date.

Michael and Kristina had a little weed welcome kit waiting for me at their house. They weren't avid users themselves, but like most people of taste and sophistication in Free America, they had a little supply on hand. They gave me a pipe, a lighter, and a couple of strains from which to choose. That would be my snack weed for a few days.

Meanwhile, I explored. At that strange bubble moment in time, you could neither buy nor sell marijuana in Oregon except for medical purposes. But you could consume it in public and share it with friends. Marijuana was well and truly free. That sounded like my dream world. The only thing

I liked better than getting high was getting high without paying money.

I read an article about a cannabis cultivator who featured a smoking tent at his wedding, featuring a massive marijuana bar and an edible buffet. Someone else told me about a marijuana-themed Fourth of July party called "Americannabis." They labeled all the infused treats and the kids had to be gone by 10:00 p.m.

Because I didn't have a wedding invitation in hand, and the Fourth of July had passed, I went first to the World Famous Cannabis Café. I paid a $10 "club fee" to get in and entered a large room, as I later described it in my *Cannabist* article, "with only intermittent art, a stage with drums and guitars, and lots and lots of tables and chairs." The word I neglected to use at the time was "dump." It was a relic from urban America's pre-artisanal past, with semi-dirty floors and bathrooms. The place felt like a rec room for people that society didn't want. And that made sense, because the owner had conceived of the café as a community center for people in trouble: disabled veterans, AIDS patients, and other marijuana-related societal outcasts.

That owner, Madeline Martinez, had a huge hand in writing Oregon's pot laws. She told me that she felt marijuana was a birthright, not a commodity. Along those lines, they had set up a "dab bar" along a wall. *Dabbing* involves heating up highly concentrated THC crystals and vaping the result. You put a little bit of paste on some glass, fire it up, and suck down the battery-acid vapor. It's one step away from cooking weed on a spoon. I might as well have been taking a hit off a crack pipe. I dabbed a few times. My lungs burned with chemicals and I coughed hard enough to dislodge a rib. Soon enough, my eyeballs went numb.

The place was full of very stoned regulars, people of all ages and backgrounds and levels of disability looking very stoned, as well as Martinez herself, who sat at a table doing dabs underneath a hand-painted sign that bore her name. A table of dudes worked on their computers, happily dabbing and answering email. "It's somewhere you can get stoned, eat some food, do a little work," one of them told me. "That's a place I want to be."

It's where I wanted to be, too. I stayed there for nearly two hours, sharing dirty mouthpieces, not talking to anyone, nursing a Coke Zero, and staring at my phone. It was a glorious time of revolution.

Oregon closed the World Famous Cannabis Café a few months later for violating the state's indoor air-quality laws.

● ● ●

That night, I went to a party. We parked the car at a train track; I'd brought along a writer friend from the old days. He and I got out and stretched our legs. We'd gotten a little stoned back at his house, but it was wearing off after the thirty-minute drive from Portland. Several other people joined us at the train track, approaching warily like deer at dusk.

"Are you here for the pot party?" one of them said, as though they couldn't believe it was possible that such a thing existed.

Down at the river, at the end of the pier, was a house larger than most of the others. The door opened, and we went inside.

The pot party was in full swing. The host, Laurie Wolf, was a New Yorker in her late fifties, but she'd relocated to Portland permanently. She also wrote recipes for *The Cannabist* sometimes. She bustled about preparing trays of delicious local meats and cheeses, as well as all kinds of sandwiches and snacks and pickles and a tasty-looking rib roast. Neatly labeled nearby were many marijuana edibles of extremely high quality, including stuffed mushroom caps with the label "Contains Cannabis. Mushroom Caps. About 5 (milligrams)

THC each," red velvet cupcakes containing 5 THC, and most delicious and deadly of all, the 25 THC baklava.

"I have a professional's tolerance," I thought about myself. But I decided to pace my consumption, popping only a mushroom cap stuffed with premium marijuana-infused breadcrumbs and ham immediately upon entering. Just about anyone can handle 5 mg.

Laurie laid out most of the goods on a dining table in the kitchen. There was more food, along with a full beverage service, in the house's main room—a big-beamed wooden retro fantasy with full Willamette River dockside access, a sort of dream home for Boomers who are still hippies at heart. Fleetwood Mac's "Rhiannon" played on the sound system.

People milled about, dabbing, loading a bowl occasionally. Everyone was very friendly and intelligent. I met a naturopathic doctor and people who ran extraction labs. There were painters and writers and entrepreneurs, political activists and people who simply loved weed. Laurie bustled among them like a stoner den mother. In 2017, the *New Yorker* would refer to her as "the Martha Stewart of marijuana edibles."

Laurie Wolf threw a series of monthly dinners for rising stars in the marijuana industry. She was a co-collaborator in a new cookbook, *Herb: Mastering the Art of Cooking with Cannabis*, and there was a lot on the line for her. If this were a different story, one about the delightful evolution of marijuana in America, meeting her would have been a magical moment for me. I just wanted to get as high as possible.

Soon, I was drooling over the buffet and blathering on to a beautiful naturopath, Dr. Shena Vander Ploeg, who would later go on to found her own line of medicinal THC-based botanicals.

"You can really taste the cannabis in this stuff," I said. "It tastes like Oregon."

"Yeah, definitely," she said.

"The French have a word for it," I said. "*Terroir.*"

"*Terroir,*" she repeated.

"*Terroir,*" I said again.

It was the marijuana equivalent of the Serge Gainsbourg song "*Je t'aime . . . moi non plus.*" God, I was pathetic. I'd had one mushroom cap, or maybe four, plus lots of joints and vapes and whatnot. One loses track. And then I ate a baklava, which pushed me over the edge for a while. My conversation grew abstract, containing such phrases as "infinite heart-space" and "I am so high right now."

The evening wound to a close early. Even in this glorious Summer of Free Weed, most of these grownups had to get back to their kids, or work in the morning. As the party ended, Laurie wrapped some baklava up in aluminum foil and handed it to me. It was big as a meatloaf.

"Oy!" she said. "So much baklava."

I ended up bringing it home, against all reason, through airport security, and consuming the precious cargo bit by bit. The baklava kept me high for a month.

● ● ●

That was where my *Cannabist* story ended, on that coy, charming note that wouldn't have been out of place in Laurie Wolf's *New Yorker* profile. But that's not where my night ended. My friend and I staggered back across the train tracks in the dark to my car. I wasn't in any condition to operate a Roku, much less a car. My brain felt like a bag of sand. But that's how I operated in this age of excess. I couldn't just take a little puff; I had to get stoned to the point of obliteration.

"There's someplace I've gotta take you," my writing buddy said.

We drove downtown without hitting anything or anyone and then went inside a storefront with a neon sign.

Red leather and studs were everywhere. Tattooed, naked women twirled around poles. Others walked around wearing garters and bras. It was an off night, and they seemed to outnumber the men.

"Welcome to Union Jack's," he said.

He'd taken me to a strip club. I literally had *one dollar* in my pocket, the high had mostly worn off, and all that remained was a grim dark aura of self-pity and vague regret. I was a broke and hungover house dad with bad sandals and an empty wallet. Union Jack's was the last place I wanted to be.

I slumped out to a smoking patio to see if I could mooch some weed. A woman approached me. She wore only a lacy black bra, matching panties attached to a garter belt, and low-heeled black shoes. Unlike most Portland strippers, she only had a couple of modest tattoos. Her body was young and supple, her face lightly freckled, her hair dusty. She looked good, but I wasn't available to play. I didn't pay for sex. I don't like to pay for *anything*.

"What do you say we go somewhere and have some fun?" she said.

I opened my wallet and showed her what was inside.

"Why the hell did you even come here, then?" she said.

"I don't know," I said.

"Typical fucking man, wants to come to a strip club and get a free show and doesn't even have the guts to pay for it."

"But . . ." I said. "My friend brought me."

"Asshole," she said. "My rent is *due*."

If I'd had a couple hundred bucks in my wallet, would that exchange have gone differently? I'd like to say no. Not only am I married, but I'm also extremely cheap. But who knows? I was wasted enough that I might have gone for the gold if no real immediate consequences had presented themselves. I was a bottomless pit of need and insecurity and the marijuana had turned my brain into cottage cheese. Weed removes boundaries, which meant anything could happen when I was high.

When I got back to my hosts' home a couple hours later, I opened up my nightstand drawer and saw that my weed supply had been replenished. I packed a bowl, went out to the porch, and inhaled a lungful of freedom. And then I took another.

POST-TREBEK STRESS DISORDER

After I won on *Jeopardy!* in 2013, I wanted to keep that feeling; I wanted to be a winner all the time. I invited everyone I'd ever met in Austin to a Mexican restaurant to watch my first game at 4:30 on a Tuesday. They all cringed through the first half of the show, as I almost went down in flames. "Only you would throw a party so people can watch you lose," someone said to me, as I got high outside during the commercial break.

But I won, and everyone cheered. I got hugs and high-fives and I even picked up the tab for the appetizers, which is how my friends knew that something was different. "I've never seen you happier," said a guy who'd known me for a long time. Now, being a comeback kid trivia champion was part of my identity.

I returned to my habit of smoking pot every day, sometimes five times a day. And I kept watching *Jeopardy!* But now I gave myself a new challenge. Every day at 4:20, conveniently ten minutes before the show started, I took a big hit off my vape pen. More like three big hits. I couldn't be too baked to watch *Jeopardy!* It made the half hour go by so fast, even the contestant interviews. I was so good, I thought, I could get 80 percent of the questions right while I was high.

I put together a pub-trivia team in Austin. To play on my team, you had to have been a *Jeopardy!* contestant. Like Samuel L. Jackson without an eyepatch, I assembled the trivia Avengers, and Post-Trebek Stress Disorder was born. As *Texas Monthly* wrote about us in a September 2017 article called "The Best Little Trivia Team in Texas": "Pollack had no trouble fielding an entire former contestant squad spanning ages, gender, race, and (most importantly) expertise . . . When it comes to finding *Jeopardy!* people in town, Pollack doesn't hide his dedication. 'I'm determined like Yul Brynner in *The Magnificent Seven*,' he explains." Unlike Yul Brynner, I got stoned before, during, and after every game. In my mind, that made me extra-awesome.

Geeks Who Drink, America's leading national trivia competition series, announced its next "Geek Bowl" in Denver, home of its corporate headquarters. This appealed to me for many reasons, most of them having to do with drugs.

My friend Jared Hall, an original PTSD member now relocated to another city, expressed willingness to go to Denver. Jared had participated in the *Jeopardy! Tournament of Champions*, where he'd rubbed patched elbows with super-players.

"I think I can get Julia and Ben," he said.

Victory was assured.

• • •

Julia Collins became the second-winningest *Jeopardy!* contestant when she won twenty games in a row back in 2014. Who wouldn't want to quiz with her in 2016? She was a genuine American hero! Ben Ingram won a bunch of games himself, before beating Collins and Arthur Chu in the *Tournament of Champions*. Who wouldn't want to quiz with them?

I'd gotten two big sluggers on board. Now it was up to me to pull the rest of the team together, just like Billy Beane in *Moneyball*. America's greatest strength is its diversity. I wanted a team with three men and three women, mixed age, gender, and ethnicity—a new team for a new era. I wasn't looking for tokenistic stunt-casting. Anyone on the roster would need to have a monster baseline of trivia knowledge. But no one knows everything. I wanted as diverse a range as possible.

To fill out the team, I asked a young journalist who'd appeared on *Jeopardy!* and was working for *Vanity Fair.* Though I'd never met her in person, she seemed super smart and she ticked all the boxes. Back in Austin, I'd been quizzing with another millennial, a PhD candidate who'd attended Princeton and was currently in the *Jeopardy!* contestant pool. The team ranged in age from twenty-four all the way up to me, forty-five years old. I'd assembled a group of quizzers that couldn't, under normal circumstances, be defeated.

But these weren't normal circumstances. Geek Bowl took place in Denver that year, and if there was anything I loved more than trivia competitions, it was legalized marijuana.

I got to town a full three days before the competition. My Aunt Estelle had a house in Denver, so I said I was there to see her and the family. And I did, I loved them and was always happy to see them. But really, I just wanted to go shopping for legal marijuana.

Within an hour of landing, I was at the weed store. I popped a 10-milligram THC gummy bear and established my baseline. As usual, I smoked and vaped and ate, gorging myself on Colorado's weed bounty like Henry VIII at the buffet. It didn't really occur to me that I was about to participate in a knowledge quiz, and that my brain needed to stay sharp. This was called Geeks Who Drink, not Geeks Who Take So Many Drugs That They Sweat Through Their Undershirt and Also It Feels Like There Are Tiny Knives Under Their Skin. It didn't matter to me. I was a weed addict, and I spent the next couple of days getting my legal fix.

When game day arrived I woke up early, did some yoga, and did some drugs. The *Vanity Fair* writer had gotten in from New York late the night before, so I had a coffee with her and Julia Collins and we all discussed what we were reading. The writer was reading *The Power Broker,* a 2,000-page biography of Robert Moses, the man who destroyed New York, which I thought was pretty funny given that I have seen that book on people's shelves, uncracked, for decades. She didn't find it so funny that I found it funny. Julia Collins was reading everything, but seemed mostly interested in talking about her project to encourage girls to pursue STEM careers. It didn't matter what they were reading, I thought. They were brilliant. We were going to win. I'd be a champion again!

"Hey guys," I said to two of America's leading young female intellectuals, "want to go to a marijuana store?"

They seemed hesitant.

"It's legal here!" I said, excitedly. "You can get it wherever and whenever you want. It's a miracle. It's like candy. Sometimes, it even *is* candy!"

Collins declined, but the writer, either because she was also polite or at least vaguely curious, came to a store with me.

"See," I said, jumping up and down at the counter. "They have flower, which is what you usually call weed, or they have candies, or sodas, or chocolates, or cookies, or crackers, or mints, or sprays, and some of this stuff you cook like crack and some of it you just put under your tongue and isn't this amazing?"

She didn't find it particularly amazing. I bought far more than I needed, given that I already had a ton of stuff at home and in the car and everywhere I needed to have it because it was Colorado and marijuana was everywhere, man, and we were all going to be stoned forever in Free America.

I assured her that I wasn't too stoned to drive, though I definitely was, and took her back to her Airbnb. Then I headed off to do a podcast interview for a show where a couple of local comedy hipsters talked to guests about their unlikely pop culture tastes; in other words, a podcast. My topic was the reality TV show *The Amazing Race*, which involved three of my favorite things: travel, winning lots of money, and hilarious footage of people trying to get donkeys to do stuff. In order to put me at ease, the podcast hosts provided copious amounts of marijuana. I smoked several strains and talked very enthusiastically with them for more than an hour. Then I bought an enormous roast beef sandwich and headed over to the Airbnb where the female members of my team were staying. Greatness called.

Jared was already there and they were all talking and having a good time. I gorged into my sandwich. To warm up, we listened to music and tried to name the song and the artist. They were all singing together, in a nice harmony. *My trivia children*, I thought. We were going to win, and we were going to do it with love.

I had a large chocolate-coconut ball full of THC in my pocket.

"Does anyone want a taste of this?" I said. "Come, come sample the bounty of the land!"

No one did. I ate the entire thing. It contained enough marijuana to sedate a horse.

Julia and Ben showed up. Ben held a bottle of Jim Beam.

"I'm from South Carolina," he said, with a heavy drawl. "This is what rebels drink." He took a monster swig of whiskey and began to sing:

For Right is strong and God has power—
The South shall rise up Free!

Every unhappy trivia family, as it turned out, is unhappy in its own way.

● ● ●

We walked to the University of Denver hockey arena, where Geek Bowl would be taking place. The air was warm and pleasant. Ingram sang Confederate songs for a mile and a half, weaving around the sidewalk.

It also became clear that, though they made the trip, Collins and Ingram weren't particularly interested in playing. After all, they'd already climbed the summit of Mount Trivia and won hundreds of thousands of dollars between them. Unlike me, they were just there to have fun and didn't have anything to prove. Only I, completely wasted on pot and driven by personal flaws that were apparent to everyone but me, felt like nothing mattered but winning. I'd drawn innocent victims into my narcissistic bubble, my quiz show passion play. And I was no longer writing the script.

"The South will rise again!" Ingram shouted.

We sat at a round plastic table off to the side of the stage. Since I'd first started playing Geek Bowl, the composition of teams had changed. You still had the groups of hard-core club trivia people from El Paso or Las Vegas or Little Rock or wherever, but 2016 was also the year that the idea of the "super team" had risen. In other words, I wasn't the only guy who'd stacked his team with *Jeopardy!* super-champions. And those super-champions weren't staggering around the arena floor, waving a bottle of smuggled-in whiskey and tossing random insults at non-white players. As Ingram blathered on, saying, "Who cares about answering a bunch of stupid liberal trivia questions," the rest of us just stared miserably at the floor, not responding to statements like "Long live Robert E. Lee!"

Needless to say, Ingram didn't perform up to his usual standards, though he did somehow manage, while sitting at the table seemingly asleep, his head nodding on his chest, to rouse himself, grab a pen, and correctly identify the song clip being played onstage by a Mexican heavy metal band as Steely Dan's "Peg."

Basically down a player, and in a bad mood, the team did okay, but not amazingly. Then came the round of doom. A paper bag appeared at each team's table to open when given a signal. The bag held eight scented penis-shaped candles, as well as a list of possible smells. We had to choose which dick candle smelled like which scent, such as Brut, Chardonnay, and Nacho Cheese. We had four minutes.

While I'll admit there was something pretty hilarious about seeing demure intellectuals frantically smelling nacho cheese-scented dick candles in a hockey arena, no one's elite education had prepared them for this task. And Ingram was asleep. We bombed it, and it didn't look like we were going to recover.

After seven rounds, we were buried somewhere like twenty-second place. Not bad, really, considering there were more than 200 teams playing, but it wasn't good enough for me. Ingram nodded in and out of consciousness. *He's ruined everything,* my inner voice was saying. Three days of drugs had worn out my brain, and I couldn't think clearly. No longer happy wasted, I sat in my chair and seethed. Jared, who knew me pretty well, looked worried. "Fuckin' Yankees," Ingram said, "and their stupid quiz questions. Who cares?"

With that, Mount Pollack erupted.

"SHUT THE FUCK UP!" I shouted.

Two seats away from me, Jared, his eyes wide, was waving his hands, and mouthing the words "no, no, no."

I stood up and pointed my finger at Ingram's chest.

"YOU FUCKING ASSHOLE!" I said. "I worked for MONTHS to put this team together, and you DESTROYED everything! It may not matter to you if you win or not, but not everybody is a MILLIONAIRE! FUCK YOU, YOU DRUNK, RACIST SON OF A BITCH!"

I threw my chair across the room.

"SHIT GODDAMMIT IT FUCK FUCK FUCK!" I shouted.

I stormed away up the stairs, out of the arena. Upstairs, I put my hands on my knees and breathed hard. Well, I'd handled that skillfully. Immediately, I started getting texts: "Come back, Neal." "He's sorry." I seethed, humiliated. I hadn't been wrong, necessarily. He had been acting like a total buffoon, but by blowing up, I'd ceded the moral high ground. I'd made it all about me and my behavior and my needs and my goals. Just like a true narcissist, just like a true addict.

I came back down the stairs, my head low, sat back down at the table, and proceeded to trudge through the final round with my miserable team of trivia ringers. "Sorry, sorry," Ingram mumbled. "You're a good man."

By no means was I a good man, but I appreciated the apology. The scores came out. We finished seventeenth.

"Not so bad," I said to my friend from Austin.

"After what *you* did?" she said. "To say something like *that*? Pathetic."

We never quizzed together again. The *Vanity Fair* writer also drifted out of the arena. I ran into her at a dinner in New York a few years later, told her I'd reformed, and she seemed relieved. Julia Collins shook my hand and said good night, professional as usual. Jared gave me a hug. Ingram also shook my hand, and early the next week he friended me on Facebook and sent me a nice message and apologized again. We've been in intermittent contact ever since. I think we recognized something in common that night. Sure, he was drunk, and that was obvious and reprehensible in that moment. But I'd done more drugs than everyone else in that hockey arena combined, hard to do considering I was in Colorado. Maybe my intoxication wasn't as visible, but it had caused me to really lose control, again.

The arena cleared out. I made my way back to my car, alone, ashamed and defeated. It wasn't the first time I'd completely lost my mind in public. Unfortunately, it would happen again, in an even bigger venue. And by then, my life had ceased to be funny.

MOTHER DIED TODAY

On the morning of my forty-seventh birthday, my father called from the hospital.

"I think they know what's wrong with me," he said, his voice distant and raspy.

"What's that, Dad?" I said.

"I have garbage in my heart," he said.

The night before, he hadn't felt much like eating his steak. His throat hurt. My younger sister Rebecca, who, along with her three kids, had been staying with my parents while she had renovations done on her house, knew something was wrong. The next morning, Dad went to the emergency room, condition unclear.

He hadn't been having heart problems. The doctors thought he had some sort of pericardial infection that had spread to his throat. As it turned out, the doctors were wrong. No one ever figured out exactly what had happened. Regardless, Dad was very sick.

"Okay, Dad," I said. "You take care of yourself."

"I just wanted to say, 'Happy Birthday,'" he croaked.

"That's fine, Dad," I said. "It's just another day."

My dad had been a diabetic for my entire adult life. He'd had bladder cancer, twice. One time his doctor had told me, "Your dad is my number-one candidate for a stroke." There had been constant scares and health problems for a decade. It was a miracle he'd made it this far; he was seventy-four years old and subsisted mainly on a diet of fatty meat protein, various pills, and—even though it was strictly forbidden—ice cream.

A few hours later, my wife and son and I went out for dinner. I had a burger and a michelada. There's a photo on the fridge of me sipping my drink, smiling, looking bright-eyed, in my final moments of happiness.

The next morning, my wife was teaching at college, and my son was at middle school, probably napping at his desk. I was sitting up in bed in my pajamas, puffing on my marijuana vape pen and watching YouTube. You know, "working."

My sister called again.

"They moved Dad to the ICU," she said.

"Oh," I said.

"He wants to see you."

Well, this was it.

I'd prepared for his death hundreds of times in my mind. Also in my mind, I was prepared to be the man of the family, to go to Arizona and comfort my mother and my sisters, all of whom could take care of themselves but all of whom needed me right now. What a man I would be.

Ten minutes later, I packed a suitcase, buzzed out of my wits. Twenty minutes later, I charged a plane ticket to Phoenix on my credit card. Regina came home from work, drove me to the airport, and I was in Arizona before sunset, still stoned.

I took an Uber to the hospital, where Rebecca was waiting for me at the ICU with Dad. He lay there with a massive tube, like a vacuum, shoved down his throat. It was making a gurgling, back-washy sound. Dad was zonked.

"Well, here he is," she said.

"Here he is," I said.

I assessed the situation. Yes, Dad looked old, but his cheeks were pink, like a baby's.

"His vitals are stable," she said.

It was pretty obvious that he wasn't going to die that night.

"Let's go home," Rebecca said. "Mom wants to see you."

● ● ●

Rebecca drove me back to the house where we'd grown up, a place of memories good and bad, of well-cared-for houseplants, a TV that was tuned to Fox News, but also lots of Don Quixote memorabilia. Years before, my mom had come within a semester or so of getting her master's in Latin-American literature. She always had a thing for the Quixote. And she spoke Spanish like a native, beautifully and elegantly. The house also contained so many wedding pictures: mine, my sisters', my cousins', my second cousins', and, strangely, of my sister's ex-husband's brother's wedding. My mom loved weddings, she loved families, she loved her six grandchildren so much. There were lots of pictures of them as well.

My mom sat at the kitchen table in her nightdress, looking tired. Her ninety-three-year-old mother Maxine was still alive, in a nice little group home a few miles away. My seventy-one-year-old mom had been taking care of Maxine, my father, and Rebecca's kids while Rebecca was at work. She also got up at 4:30 every morning to hike five miles with her twitchy schnoodle, Cosmo, who my parents had named after Kramer from *Seinfeld*. So she usually looked tired around dinnertime.

"This isn't good," she said.

Like me, like all of us, she figured Dad would be dead within the week.

"There's a chocolate bar in the fridge for you," she said. "We brought it home from Colorado."

When we'd visited family there the previous summer, Mom and I went to a pot dispensary. Never a stoner, she wanted to see what all the fuss was about and bought a little candy. Then she'd saved me some for when I visited next.

"I didn't like it. I think your father has been nibbling at it a little. But it didn't do much for us."

Mom never approved of my pot habit. But she indulged it anyway once it became legal. That was true love.

My sister Margot flew in from Los Angeles to help out Mom while our dad was sick. Rebecca left to spend the night at her boyfriend's apartment. Her kids were at their dad's, and Margot and I were around for Mom. Margot slept in Rebecca's old bedroom and I slept in Margot's old bedroom, because Dad had converted mine into his office long ago. Everything had been tossed about by the decades, but I was the oldest. The family pecking order remained intact.

Mom coughed.

"I think I need to go to bed, honey," she said. "I have a little cold."

I kissed her on the forehead.

She coughed again, louder.

"You *are* sick," I said.

"It's nothing," she said.

Margot and I made her some hot tea with honey and lemon. I went to bed. Mom kept coughing. She felt a little feverish. Margot said she'd sit up with her for a while.

At 3:00 a.m., Margot appeared at my doorway.

"Mom's coughing up blood," she said.

"*What?*" I said.

I went into my parents' bedroom. Mom was staggering around on the carpet, turning in little circles.

When people have seizures, or migraines, they describe a mental shadow forming before the attack actually happens, a kind of warning that something terrible is about to occur. I felt a sort of penumbra, very strong and thick and dark, begin to gather over my entire life. While I didn't know exactly what was coming, I sensed that it would be very bad.

"Are you okay, Mom?" I said.

"I . . . need help," she said.

"We need to get her to the hospital," I said to Margot. "Now."

"Someone has to be here for Cosmo!" Margot exclaimed.

"You are kidding," I said.

"No," she said. "I'm not."

Cosmo got even *more* neurotic if he didn't get walked in the morning.

"Fine," I said.

We determined that I'd stay home and walk Cosmo in the morning. Margot drove Mom to the hospital. I went back to bed, where I lay sweating, the blanket pulled up to my face, eyes wide. What was happening?

An hour later, Margot texted.

"The hospital is ignoring Mom," Margot said. "She's in real distress. I just lost my shit on them."

"Okay," I texted back, feeling helpless. "Keep me posted."

Sleep wouldn't come so I put on a yoga video and ran through the poses. Yoga would always be there for me, no matter what. Besides, it was still dark out. There was nothing else to do. Soon after I finished, I got another text from Margot.

"Mom admitted to ICU. She's been intubated. Walk the dog."

• • •

I went to the hospital at 11:00 a.m. My Aunt Estelle arrived from Denver to look after her brother, my father. She was also my mother's best friend. She was beloved to my sisters and me, like a second mother, but with none of the baggage that comes with having a parent. So we needed her.

My parents were both in the ICU, three doors down from each other. Forty-eight hours earlier, I'd been stoned in bed, content with my lot. Suddenly, I was plunged into a supporting role in a *Lifetime* movie.

First, I went to Dad's room. Estelle was in there, talking to him gently.

"He looks pretty good," she said to me, in her practical, semi-optimistic way.

Well, he didn't look any worse than the night before. They still hadn't figured out exactly what was wrong with him, but whatever antibiotics they were pumping into his body kept things from getting worse.

The scene in my mother's room was much more grim.

She was in bed, a tube down her throat. But unlike my father, she was horribly conscious. She recognized me; her eyes glazed with terror.

"Whuuuuu," she moaned.

I held her hand.

"Just breathe, Mom," I said. "Be calm."

Margot and I tried to get her to count her breath.

"In, two-three-four," I said. "Out, two-three-four."

Mom tried to follow along with my yoga and meditation nonsense. But she couldn't breathe. She couldn't do anything. I could provide no comfort.

How could this have happened? My mother was an exercise *nut*. She warmed up with 10,000 steps, then went to the gym, and then she got 10,000 more. When she was about my age, maybe a little older, Mom had some sort of nerve problem in her neck. For a few weeks, she lost the use of her legs. We figured she'd be in a wheelchair for the rest of her life. A few months later, she was climbing mountains.

To see her so helpless like this simply crushed me. No one supported me more totally than my mother. She'd always been part of my life, no matter how strange that life became, even though I lived 1,000 miles away.

I could tell Mom anything, and I usually did. Mom's presence gave me confidence and courage and hope. "You are my heart and soul," she'd told me one time.

And now she was rotting away before my eyes.

Margot coughed.

I looked at my sister. Her eyes were bloodshot. Her face had turned gray. She was sweating and sniffling.

"Jesus Christ," I said. "What is *wrong* with you?"

"I feel terrible," she said.

Had some sort of terrible plague gotten into the air vents of my boyhood house? Was it killing my entire family? Was I next?

I called my boyhood friend, Gregg Tolliver, who's now an infectious disease doctor in California. Among other assignments, he'd been in charge of trying to stem the outbreak of tuberculosis at San Quentin Prison. I told him what was going on.

"Your sister needs to get on a prophylaxis immediately," he said. "And you need to take one of hers until you get your own prescription."

"Are you kidding?" I said.

"You have forty-eight hours," he said.

We left Aunt Estelle with my mother, who was still writhing in terror and agony, and went to the emergency clinic to get Margot her drugs. My cousin Liz texted me.

"This is bad," she said.

"No kidding," I said.

Margot took her drugs, and we went home where we met Rebecca. She had a substantial supply of Clorox wipes. We swabbed down every surface of the kitchen and the bathrooms, and all the seats of both my parents' cars. My dad's ancient SUV wouldn't have gotten clean if we'd used a Navy-issue power washer. But we Cloroxed it anyway.

We laundered all the sheets and Rebecca ordered a cleaning service to fumigate the house the next morning. None of that would matter, though, if we were Family Zero for some sort of real-life Captain Trips, the virus that wiped out most of humanity in Stephen King's *The Stand*. Maybe I'll survive this, I thought. Maybe I'll be the one who makes it to the showdown with the Dark Man in Vegas.

Estelle texted from the hospital that both my parents were stable. I ordered a pizza, picked it up, and ate the entire thing by myself at the kitchen table in about five minutes. Margot took drugs and went to bed.

I walked the dog around the block and then I went to bed. I put my phone on Do Not Disturb, the most selfish act in my supremely selfish life, Margot sent me several texts overnight, asking me to bring her Advil and water, and I snoozed peacefully through all of them. Eventually, she crawled off her air mattress and dragged herself down the hall to the bathroom to help herself.

"I didn't have a choice!" she said the next morning.

She looked better. It appeared our plague predictions had proved inaccurate. Our house was not the scene of a sequel to *Outbreak*.

We had a good laugh.

After Margot and I left, Rebecca visited my mother.

"I don't want to die," Mom said. "Please don't let me die."

It was the last thing she said to Rebecca, or anyone.

● ● ●

I got to the hospital by 11:00 a.m. My Aunt Estelle had been sitting by my dad's side all morning, when she wasn't with my mom. Dad looked pretty much the same, even a little bit better. My mom, on the other hand, was lying still and gray and waxy, the tube pumping air into her lungs. Whatever fight she'd shown the previous day had gone. Mother had become a mummy.

"She'll be okay," Aunt Estelle said. "She's a fighter."

But I knew she was wrong.

I knew it was over.

At noon, my high-school friend showed up at the hospital with a packet of THC gummies from a medical-marijuana dispensary. I'd placed the order soon after landing in Phoenix, figuring I'd need drugs to get through the anxiety of the week, not knowing I'd be dealing with more than mere anxiety. I popped one. It was strong, too strong. Soon enough, I felt completely zonked.

Upstairs, they'd enclosed my mother in a tent. Whatever battle Mom was fighting, she was now fighting it alone, though there were still people working on her behalf. A team of Air Force nurses, who were training at the hospital, buzzed around her like she had a belly full of shrapnel. I'd never seen so many devices and tubes. I could only watch, like she was some sort of exhibit in a medical museum.

Around 1:00 p.m., the doctor pulled me aside.

"Your mother had a lung infection," she said. "It was dormant. And then she got pneumonia, and it burst. The infection spread throughout her entire body. We're going to try to a few more things."

Inside the room, six people turned knobs and pumped fluids, desperately trying to save my mother's life.

I called my sisters, who were out running errands.

"What's up?" said Rebecca.

"You need to get down here," I said.

Five minutes later, the doctor said to me, "If you want a spiritual leader, you need to ask for one now."

"Can we get a rabbi?" I asked.

It was Saturday morning. The rabbis all had other things to do. My sisters arrived.

"I just asked for a rabbi," I said.

They both started to sob.

My aunt rushed out from my dad's room. He was also intubated and unconscious, maybe 200 feet from where my mother was dying. Nothing had prepared me for this. My glorious five-decade adolescence was over. The lights came on. The party had ended, now just an empty, trash-strewn room.

"This can't be happening!" Estelle cried. "This isn't real! It's like something from a horror movie!"

The doctor approached us.

"We've done everything we can," she said. "If we take the tube out, it'll be a matter of minutes."

My sisters and I looked at one another. We were all sobbing. And we nodded.

"Do it," I said.

Margot called her cantor in Los Angeles. He told us to gather around my mother's body, and to hold hands. The Sh'ma, he said, is the most sacred prayer of the Jewish faith. When chanted around the body of a dying person, it would carry them up to heaven. He began, and we chanted along with him, voices choking:

Sh'ma Yisrael
Adonai Eloheinu
Adonai E'Chad

All the while, I was thinking: This is a *little* Jewy for me. But it was what my mother would have wanted.

Five minutes later, she was dead.

I went into the corridor, sat on the ground, and buried my head in my hands. That's what you're supposed to do when your mom dies suddenly, right? I called my wife and son to let them know. They were sobbing. Everyone was sobbing. We'd all sob all the time, from now on.

"What the *fuck*?" my son said.

"I don't know," I said.

The hospital had brought us a sad-looking tray of fruits and snacks.

"Get those out of here!" Margot cried. "I'm not hungry!"

"I have gummies," I said pathetically to the nurses, who did not care about my drug habit. "I'm going to need them."

Rebecca stayed behind to take care of some paperwork and look in on Dad, who was doing better. Margot drove us back to the house, which was full of Mom's stuff—her art, her books, her jewelry, her clothes, her dog, her spirit. Neighbors had arranged for a full-catered array of deli food. Friends of Rebecca's sat at the kitchen table, eating it. One of her friends was in the dining room, taping a blanket over the mirrors, because apparently that's a Jewish custom when somebody dies. But I'd had just about enough of stupid Jewish death rituals for one day.

"Take that goddamn blanket down!" I shouted. "NOW!"

I scarfed some deli in the kitchen while making conversation with friends of my sisters who I'd never met before. Who *were* these people?

"I taped *Young Frankenstein* on Turner Classic Movies," I said, idly. "Maybe I'll watch it later."

They looked at me with pity. I slurped my matzo ball soup, baked out of my wits. Mother was dead, but at least I had corned beef and latkes.

Soon, Rebecca came over. Her fiancé showed up and everyone had a good cry and hug. Then finally, they all left. Margot and I looked at each other. Her family was in Los Angeles, mine was in Austin. They'd show up soon. But for now, Margot and I remained in the house where we'd grown up and loathed each other most of the time.

"This is my worst nightmare," she said.

"Mine, too," I said.

I got into the shower and turned the water onto maximum hot. Placing my head against the tile, I started to cry, alone.

What am I going to do? I thought.

From down the hall, I heard Margot moan. She shared my melodramatic tendencies.

"I want my mommy!" she cried. "I want my mommy!"

•••

My mom had shriveled up and died before my eyes in fewer than thirty-six hours. She was in the ground almost as quickly. "Jews bury fast," Aunt Estelle said.

Even though the doctors said Dad was probably well enough to come out of sedation, we decided to keep him under for a couple days longer. There was a lot to do. Fortunately, my sisters are both professional event planners. They sat at the dining room table, making calls. Florists were dispatched, catering arranged. They even found a flamenco guitarist.

After a few hours spent frantically rummaging through my father's desk, we found out all the papers were in order. We spent twelve hours on and off hold with the VA. Dad had arranged for a dual plot for himself and Mom at the veterans' cemetery in North Scottsdale. The military provided that free of charge. She'd had a small life insurance policy, which took care of the funeral expenses. My sisters put everything on their credit cards and got paid back later. I didn't pay a dime. Spending money on anything literally fills me with physical pain. I am not claiming to be a quality person. Regardless, my parents had been properly bankrolled for death.

This took away one category of stress for me. Many more remained. While my sisters worked the phones, I could barely summon the energy to fold a towel. My uselessness can't be overstated. I just smoked pot and stared blankly at the cacti.

Mom's funeral was on a Monday morning. I stayed up all night, doing whatever my version of praying looked like, mostly sitting on my heels on the floor and feeling sorry for myself while Regina gently snored in the adjacent bed. At 8:00 a.m., I put on my only suit: a blue-and-white pinstriped

Armani that I'd bought for a friend's wedding fourteen years before. It still looked pretty fresh. I don't have a lot of occasions to put on pants during the day, much less a shirt and tie. Now, I had a bad reason.

My sisters and I met with my mother's rabbi in a side office of a fraying building in Central Phoenix that looked and smelled like an old knish. Margot, Rebecca, and I had never met him before, but he seemed to know our mom pretty well. He was as shocked as anyone, though not so shocked that he couldn't resist telling us about the cruise he'd just gotten back from. He was eighty years old, at least, and had a large bandage on his forehead where he'd recently had some sort of growth removed. A few months later, he would be expelled from the temple for sending creepy notes to a congregant. We told him we wanted to speak at the service, but he made it clear that he was running the show and would be delivering a sermon as well. We were in no mood to fight.

We emerged from the office and I found myself wrapped in the embrace of former neighbors and dinner partners of my parents, several of my former high school teachers, and friends of my sisters who I'd barely known. There were cousins and step-cousins. My former nanny, Debbie, who'd come from England to take care of my sisters and me during my family's flush years in the late seventies, had flown a long way to say goodbye to the woman who'd changed her life. Random *alte kakers* threw pitying glances my way. My body felt hot and prickly. My head was full of wasps.

The place filled up fast. If it had been a weekend, we would have needed an overflow room. When I saw how many people had turned out for Mom's funeral, I realized that I wasn't the only one who'd known how special she'd been. My mother's life had meaning. People wanted to say goodbye to her. But I didn't.

As the service began the rabbi droned, telling a joke that my mom's age, seventy-one, had made her "practically a teenager in Phoenix." This was true, and actually kind of funny. I sat in the front row, next to my wife and son, nervously fingering my note card.

I took over the podium from the rabbi, wearing my only suit and a venue-provided black yarmulke that shot up like a dunce cap over my big, shiny forehead, accented with a black ribbon on my left lapel and a monster beard that I shaved off a few months later. A white ceramic vase full of daisies—Mom's favorite—accented with purple baby's breath, stood to my left. Behind me, hanging on the wall with its mediocre stucco job, was some sort of ugly Jewish-themed weave art.

My eyes were raw and red and my voice heavy with sorrow.

"Good morning everyone. I'm Neal. Believe it or not. Susan's first born and her only son. I just want to say on behalf of my sisters, from the bottom of our hearts we want to thank you for coming here to pay tribute to our mother. It is overwhelming, the amount of support and love we've received from family and friends. It is really touching to know how much and how well our mother was loved by so many. We thank you so much for everything you brought to her. And to us.

"I guess we have to talk about it. Our father is in intensive care. That's the bad news. He is sedated. He does not know that his wife passed. When he went under, she was fine. He is, however, getting better. He's showing improvement, and he's got a chance. Which is a miracle, as far as I'm concerned. So whatever higher power you pray to, say a prayer to that power for Bernie. 'Cause we want to see our dad again."

Here, I teared up, understandably.

"We really didn't get to say goodbye to our mother, so we'd like to say goodbye to him. Or even hello. Hello would be nice! Let's say hello. Let's start with hello. If I went in and said goodbye to him, he'd live another ten years just to spite me."

The crowd laughed at that. I had broken the ice, and I could begin the tribute.

"All right. My mother . . . My sisters and I sort of have a division of labor here. We're going to talk about different aspects of her life. I decided not to prepare something formal because it was going to be pretentious. And frankly, I was pretty tired. So I'm going to talk off the cuff.

"I wanted to talk about my mother as an intellectual. She was just a brilliant, brilliant woman. More than anyone else, she was someone with whom I could share books, and recommendations for books. And unlike most people, the books she recommended to me were usually pretty good. She had wonderful taste, and always had an interesting opinion, even if I didn't totally agree with it. If I sent her a book that had, say, adult themes, she would comment on that drily and move on.

"She was always reading. Ever since I was small, she'd have a book in her hand and made sure I had a book in my hand, too. I've had so many long—probably longer than she would have wanted—conversations with her about books. It just went on and on. It continued, it continued up until, well, it was my birthday a week ago. We talked for a good long while about many, many things. Especially about what we were reading. And I'll miss that so much.

"She sent me a birthday card. All the jokes were things that she'd seen me write about on Twitter. Full of hashtags and @'s. She wrote '#resist.' Which I thought was pretty good. Yes, mother, I'll resist, don't worry.

"You know, Susan taught me how to read. Literally. Taught me how to read. How to think. And just to love learning. In retrospect, though, maybe someone else should have taught me how to drive. That was not her greatest skill."

This got a good laugh. Everyone knew how bad a driver my mother had been.

"What was most extraordinary about *Señora Pollack* is that she loved Latin culture so much that she thought in Spanish. In her mind, I think it was her culture even though she was a Jewish girl from New Jersey. When she spoke Spanish—you all have seen it—when she spoke Spanish, she transformed into this very magisterial and eloquent person. Not that she wasn't eloquent in English, but it was extraordinary. I just loved watching her speak Spanish. She spoke it so beautifully. Classically. She introduced me to the Quixote, and Gabriel García Márquez, and Julio Cortázar, and Isabel Allende. And made me read them in the original Spanish, which was very frustrating.

"She would say, '*Una mujer sophisticada habla Español.*' That means 'a sophisticated woman speaks Spanish.' And she *was* a sophisticated woman. She encouraged me to become a writer. Which, in the long run, probably wasn't a great financial decision. But it was the *right* decision. She spotted that in me right away. Throughout my life, she was my fiercest advocate, and my number-one fan, and a frequent commenter on my Facebook page, I might add. Everyone loved her there, too. She was so witty and so funny and played the role of mother so ironically, which was how I liked it. She was always there for me, even online.

"The thing is: At the end, she was developing a literary career herself. She translated a children's book—wait, which way did she do it?—from English to Spanish. And she was asking me questions about how to market yourself. How to find an agent, how to get it out there. She was poised for a fabulous second career. I'm so glad she got one. It's such a gift to publish a book. It's a gift she gave me. She gave me the courage to do it myself. I wish she'd gotten to publish more, but I'm so glad she got to publish one.

"She was my best friend, and my fiercest ally in life. I'll miss her terribly. And she'll always be with me. That's enough of me. I'd like to bring my sister Margot up."

My sisters both spoke, eloquently and from the heart. My son, all of fourteen years old, spoke, too, way more chill and poised than I would have been at his age. Mom was no softie. She had a wry and acid side as well. My son was the only one who'd admitted that at the funeral.

"So, when I think of my grandma, there's always this one story that comes to mind. I'm not sure why it comes to mind, but it always does, ever since it happened. When I was about six or seven, we were going on a road trip, and I was watching a movie and my headphones broke. So we pull over at this store and she buys me these really nice headphones. We get back in the car, and I try them on after like an hour, and I say, 'They're not very comfortable.' I took them off and I refused to wear them. She turns around and looks at me and says, 'Seriously?'"

He shook his head in imitation of her and got a nice big laugh. He had inherited my penchant for comic timing, but also had a cute mop of curly blond hair.

"And I think the reason it stuck with me is because she did something so nice for me, and I didn't appreciate it. Now, I really appreciate it."

He put his hand over his heart.

"When I decided not to get bar mitzvahed, I was afraid that she'd get angry at me or that it would change the way she treated me. It didn't at all. She treated me exactly the same. And it really meant a lot to me. As one of her grandkids, I can say she loved us more than anything. She even said to me one time, when I was visiting, 'I'm happy to see your parents, but I'm *really* happy to see you.'"

With that laugh line, Elijah slipped away from the podium. I loved my son for his honesty. What a *mensch*.

It was all over soon after that. People hugged me and offered sympathies. I surreptitiously popped a gummy, turned to my son and my niece, and said, "Let's get the hell out of here."

Afterward, everyone my parents had ever known came over for brunch at the house. I'd told my son and my niece to hang around and keep me amused, then I ate two more gummies. I gave one to my cousin and later, I saw him sitting on a couch, staring at the wall. His tolerance was not as high as mine.

"I need to talk to you about these drugs," he said.

Someone did, that was for sure.

• • •

A few days later, the government lowered my mother's body into the desert. My sisters and I watched from behind a rope as the casket cranked into the ground.

"Goodbye, Mom," I said.

A biker funeral was going on simultaneously. Harleys revved in the distance. Dust blew everywhere.

"I can't believe this," Margot said.

"Let's get the hell out of here," I said.

Estelle texted us.

"They're waking up your father," she said.

At the hospital, a professional grief counselor had been employed to handle this situation. Dad's eyes were moving around, groping for clarity. I walked in. He'd already seen my sisters.

"My son," he said.

"Hey Dad," I said.

"Where's Susan?" he said.

"Bernie," the counselor said. "The day after you went into the hospital, Susan got very sick. She had a lung infection, it burst, and she died, very quickly. Your kids were all with her, and so was your sister."

My dad exhaled.

There were tears in his eyes.

"Sonofabitch," he said.

My sentiments exactly.

● ● ●

The day after my mother died, her brother, Rick, went to the home to tell Maxine, their mother, the news. Rick worked as a programmer for IBM in the 1970s, was instrumental in developing the software for the first automatic-teller machines, and then had a second career as a commercial airline pilot and a Lieutenant Colonel in the Civil Air Patrol. He once advised me to "suck off the beautiful tit of life." That's what you want from an uncle. He'd been planning to stay with my folks in Phoenix while he got his shoulder replaced. But my entire family had collapsed at once and for now, his surgery was on hold.

"Where's Susan?" Grandma asked.

There was no way to sugarcoat it.

"Oh nooo!" she cried.

The owner of the home and her husband comforted my grandmother while Uncle Rick stood by. I left the room for a few minutes and when I came back in, she had recovered, or at least had been sedated.

"Richard?" she said.

"Yes, ma?" said Uncle Rick.

"Can you get me a latte from McDonald's?"

"What?"

"I want a latte from McDonald's. I saw it on TV."

Uncle Rick went into the kitchen and poured a mug of coffee for his mother and put a little milk in it.

"Is this from McDonald's?"

"Sure, Grandma," I said.

"Well," she said. "Susan is gone. But I'm still here. I'm not at death's door myself."

"Okay, Mom," Rick said.

"You can't figure death," she said, sipping her coffee through a straw.

Three months later, she was dead too.

● • ●

My father recovered and spent the summer in Colorado with my extended family. Aunt Estelle made sure he ate healthy and got plenty of exercise. By Thanksgiving, he was a little lonely but basically back to normal.

We all did what we could to get him better. In April, I went back to Phoenix to take care of him for a week. His throat still hadn't healed entirely, so he had to drink thickened liquids. He didn't have much of an appetite, either, and wasn't able to drive.

One night, he broiled some steaks. He and I sat at the kitchen table, grousing at each other.

"What time is the Dodger game on?" I asked.

He slammed down his fork.

"You want to watch the fucking Dodger game?" he shouted. "Watch it. Watch it. WATCH IT!"

I'd been dealing with these random rage eruptions my entire life and eventually, I'd found marijuana to help me cope. On this night, though, I fought back.

"You think I'm not grieving too, old man?" I said. "You don't get to talk to me like that!" That shut him up.

Outside, Cosmo was making some sort of ruckus. I heard a terrifying *EEP!* sound. Cosmo was scuffling under a planter, looking for something.

I shooed the dog inside. A newborn bird lay on the tile, gasping for breath, its eyes closed. I held it in my palm and stroked its chest.

"It's going to be okay," I said. "You rest now. It's all right."

I walked out onto the lawn, petting a little bird that had been born just to be murdered by my dead mother's beloved dog. Life was brutal and short and unfair and suffering was the only reality, so I tried to show that baby bird the only kindness it had never known.

And then it died in my hand. I walked over to the back wall of my parents' yard.

"Fuck it," I said.

I flung the baby bird's corpse into the desert. It would be worth two in the bush.

I went back inside and washed my hands.

"What was that about?" Dad asked.

"Never mind," I said.

I resumed grimly eating my broiled Brussels sprouts across from my father, who was alive. He and I regarded each other warily, like the survivors of some sort of terrible attack who'd been thrown together against their wishes. I'd expected to be left with only one parent at some point, but I'd expected it to be the *other* parent. Mom and I will grow old together, I'd thought. I will take care of her just like she took care of me. Now that story would never be told.

Dad loved me in his way and wanted me to be happy and successful, but he had his own problems that made mine look no harder than a Monday crossword. As the months rolled along, those problems would grow worse. He would not, and could not, serve as my rock in my hour of greatest emotional need.

So what's next? I thought.

As it turned out, the answer was: a lot of drugs.

THE HAND YOU'RE DEALT

A few weeks after Mom died, my friend Zack sent me a GChat message inviting me to a free poker tournament at a shitty chicken-wing bar called Sidelines. Sidelines was like a bar out of the apocalypse. It anchored the street-side slot of a massive strip mall on a busy boulevard in Cedar Park, Texas, befouling the landscape with cheap banners advertising happy hour, enticing divorced men to come in and watch the Cowboys. While Sidelines may have called itself a "sports grille," it was really a cheap-beer troll hut that kept its clientele sedated with video gambling and various "sweepstakes."

Zack was fifteen years younger and liked to describe himself as my "#1 Fan." After a few months on the poker circuit with me, that was downgraded to "begrudging ally." If you invite a vampire into your house, you have to deal with the consequences.

"Okay," I said, sealing my fate. "That sounds fun."

I descended into a swirl of addiction and poor judgment, forcing the people who still loved me to suffer more than usual. I placed my marriage in mortal danger while I pursued drugs and low-rent gambling, extracurricular activities that would have seemed immature for a man twenty-five years younger than I was. But the addict wants what he wants, and nothing will stand in the way of his pleasures, especially not his family. I didn't care that my behavior steadily chipped away at the foundations of the modest home life that I'd carefully built over the last twenty years. Domesticity and emotional honesty didn't have much appeal. I *wanted* to be a hairy, thrashing man-baby. My mom was dead. It made me reckless.

The grief was like an insane low-grade buzzing in the back of my head. I wanted to fill that space with whatever I could to drown out the noise and the pain. So that's what I did, all summer long. I desperately needed a distraction. "Immerse yourself in work," said a friend who was also mourning a recently dead parent. But that's never been my style. My goal in life is to work less.

By then, my editor had left *The Cannabist*, and the site had become just another marijuana-related content aggregator. I was no longer a marijuana journalist, but I still had all the swag. In the mornings, with my cup of coffee, I'd charge up my little vape pen, bring the coffee cup to my lips, blow the vapor into it, and re-inhale it with my second gulp of coffee. Repeat this ritual once or twice, and I was good and jacked to start the day.

By midmorning, I was ready for another round of vape hits. Around lunch, I'd eat a gummy or a candy or some other cannabis snack, assuming I had some around. When things started to lag midafternoon, I'd switch to flower and load a handsome bowl, walk outside to the back deck and take a huge stinky hit, swatting mosquitoes while listening to the birds chirp and the airplanes blast and the summer bugs croak.

In between moments of consumption, I did anything to avoid the twin devils of working or dealing with my feelings. I'd tinker with my fantasy baseball team, or watch movies, or futz with email, or do a little yoga.

When it came time for *Jeopardy!* at 4:30, I fired up my desktop vaporizer—my beloved Silver Surfer—and vaped a nub until it was black. Then I struggled to play along with Trebek. I took a few more hits before dinner and sat at the table with my family, head nodding down to my chest.

The spiritual journey didn't call me either. On Mother's Day, I went to a yoga class at my local studio.

"We are all mothers," the teacher said.

"My mother is dead," I said.

Later, as I grumped in child's pose, she touched me gently on the back and said, "I'm here for you." Then she turned to the class and said, "Bow to your inner mother."

So yoga was out for the time being. I needed a new mental challenge that would absorb me completely. It had to be very time-consuming, fun, and sleazy. It was time to go play poker.

Poker fit every category. It would also eventually become an addiction as toxic as, if not more than, marijuana.

I walked into Sidelines on a bright and sunny spring day and entered a dank, blue-lit miasma. TVs covered every open inch of wall, spewing all manner of sports garbage. The place smelled like old chicken and stale Budweiser, with a faint undercurrent of sewage and despair. A layer of vape smoke wafted in from the outdoor patio. I made my way to the back, where, catty-corner to the overflowing toilets, the poker room awaited.

There were three tables covered in felt that had obviously seen a lot of action. On busy nights, I'd later learn, the tournament would leak into the main barroom. They'd throw rubber mats on top of tall tables and players would sit on stools, hunched over their cards and their beers, plotting their next moves.

Without paying a penny, I put my name on a sign-in sheet. And, with that, I'd joined the Texas Fantasy Poker League. The tournament director said, "You can sit anywhere."

There were stacks of chips at every seat. As a first-time player, I got an extra $5,000 orange chip. Not like it mattered. I was going to lose them all quickly.

The TFPL was hardly the pinnacle of poker competition. "When this league started fifteen years ago, it was like 70 percent good players, maybe 30 percent who didn't know what they were doing," a lifer later told me. "Now, it's like 30-70. Or maybe 10-90."

But whether the players were good or not, I was at the back of the sandbox that first night. Playing in the TFPL not only required knowing what makes a good poker hand—which I didn't, not really—but also knowing how to deal, shuffle, and count chips. When the poker is free, the players do all the work. It also helped if you understood the structure and pacing of a poker tournament. Unsure of what I was doing, I leaked chips for about an hour and a half before going bust. But it was more fun than grieving.

The League offered freeroll Texas Hold'em tournaments around town seven nights a week. One of them took place at a chicken-wing bar called Fowler's, about a twelve-minute drive from my house, so close I didn't even have to get on the highway. One night soon after our first tournament, Zack and I went to Fowler's to check out the scene. I got high in the parking lot, as usual, and then I descended into hell.

In many ways, Fowler's was the same bar as Sidelines, clinging to existence via various specials and gimmicks. As opposed to Sidelines' dank-gray cave motif, Fowler's went for more of a brown-and-yellow neon grimness. But though they were equally filth-and-swill-ridden, Fowler's had a somewhat more friendly vibe, and marginally more edible food. The good-looking staff did shots with customers. Whereas Sidelines felt like an outpost bar on a prison planet, Fowler's felt like a place where sometimes people enjoyed themselves. I know I did. Sometimes.

Fowler's owed its entire existence to the Texas Fantasy Poker League. Every night, the TFPL brought in thirty to sixty customers, almost all of whom emptied their wallets into their bar tabs. Though the game itself had a free buy-in, you got extra chips by ordering food. Unless you were very lucky or very good, you needed to eat chicken wings if you wanted a shot at actually winning the tournament. A Fowler's cheeseburger tripled your stack and quadrupled your chances at arterial blockage.

To add to the absurdity, if a player went bust, they could replenish their starting stack by shouting out "GRACIOUS!" very loudly. This was league-speak for "gracious loser," meaning you had to buy another round for everyone at the table. You couldn't call it a "rebuy" because that, god forbid, would imply this was *poker gambling*—apparently against the law in the great state of Texas where the sport of Hold'em was created. The winner of the nightly tournament got a $75 kickback, the second-place finisher got $25, and a lucky number three got a $25 gift card to Fowler's—a mixed blessing. Everything else went to the house. So players graciously bought round after round, night after night, and this crew of total degenerates was able to help Fowler's pay its electric bill for another month.

From 6:30 p.m. until around midnight, the entire back half of the bar became a poker room, with plastic mats slapped onto tables, never fewer than three tables, and often up to eight. On slow nights, poker players were the *only* clientele, leaking into the booths after their near-inevitable eliminations to play dominoes or wretchedly nurse a plate of bar nachos. I soon learned that nothing was more depressing than busting out before the end of dinner. You had to pick your plate off the side tray and choke down your fries at a lonely table far from the action, remorsefully binge-eating and thinking about how it had all gone wrong.

After their shifts, the bartenders and waitresses tried their skill at the tables. The talent leaked the other way, too. Sometimes an unlucky guy came in for a freeroll, hung out for a couple of weeks, and suddenly found himself floor-managing, cadging tips off stingy old nits who screamed "I wanted *ranch dressing*" after finding their six-dollar lunch specials not to their liking.

I went bust quickly my first night at Fowler's. And my second, too. But I returned, gravitating to the bottom of the pond, seduced by the siren song of the cards. Some of my fellow players had money, others were broke as shit. There were MBAs and there were high school dropouts, people who were misshapen, handsome, drunk, sober, unemployed, white, black, Mexican, Indian, pregnant, old, underage, friendly, tolerant, bigoted, peaceful, and violent. In an unusual twist, the TFPL featured a higher-than-average number of deaf players, which meant hearing-abled players learned to use hand signals. Thrusting your thumb upward meant "raise," and "call" was a kind of hang-loose signal with pinky and thumb extended while wagging your hand. However, when the deaf player busted you out, it was still the standard handshake, followed by the standard headshake.

On nights that went well for me, I loved them all. On nights where it all went wrong, they were my most vile enemies.

Then something strange happened. One night at Fowler's, I didn't bust out. I just sat there nursing my cards, folding everything except pocket aces, pocket kings, pocket queens, and ace-king suited. This happened to be one of those nights where the cards were running hot for me. I didn't know how to play them, but I played them well enough. The other players began to vanish, drifting away like ghosts.

Suddenly, I was at the final table. Then I *really* stopped playing my cards. I nursed my tiny stack of chips like a broken drunk hovering over his final sips of whiskey. This seemed appropriate, because the chip leader, a swaggering weirdo named Bruce, was pounding back endless glasses of Wild Turkey, continually pushing his entire stack of chips into the middle, causing us all to recoil in fear. Still, I made the final four, somehow. The big blind came along, I bet my chips, and went belly-up for the weakest fourth-place finish in poker tournament history.

Still, under TFPL rules, I had qualified for points, which is what anyone in the final sixteen players got in lieu of money. It wasn't a stack of cash, but now I knew that I could compete, even if that meant just sitting there like a stone, not playing. I was Bartleby the poker player. I preferred not to.

My poker career, even though I didn't realize it at the time, had begun for real. There at the dawn of justice, I was just little Nemo whistling out into the ocean, unaware of the adventures that awaited me.

● ● ●

On those hot summer nights, I drove my 1998 Nissan Sentra to the chicken-wing bar with the overflowing toilets in search of a facsimile of poker glory. I bought a glossy card protector with the Texas Fantasy Poker League logo on one side and the Alamo Drafthouse logo on the other. This cost me $15. Every time I brought it to Fowler's or Sidelines, I got a bonus 5,000 orange chip. And I brought it a lot.

"If you don't watch yourself," Zack said to me, "you're going to become a regular at Fowler's."

His warning came too late.

To aid me in my poker quest, Zack had given me two books: one was called *Every Hand Revealed*. It featured a glowering cover photo of a bald Danish poker pro named Gus Hansen and a hand-by-hand account of how Hansen won the $1.5 million Aussie Millions tournament in 2007. I tried to read it, but I knew so little about the game that it might as well have been written in Danish.

The other was called *Catching Fish*, a self-published book about beating low-stakes poker games that had a cover illustration of a catfish wearing a suit and holding cards. That book made a little more sense to me, but it also had kind of an unpleasant tone and I found some copy-editing mistakes. So I moved ahead, blindfolded in the dark.

One night I went to Fowler's, got stoned, and played well. I don't know how, but I did. Over a few hours, the players drifted away like spirits in a mystical Miyazaki forest. Soon, there was only one other player left: a young auto mechanic named Jacob. He had a wry sense of humor and a lot of experience at the tables, including a $40,000-plus cash win at a World Series of Poker event. He played poker at Fowler's because it was a cheap night out. When players lost, which they did almost all the time, they just shrugged and said, "free poker." The zero-buy-in element took away a lot of the sting of defeat.

Jacob had a big stack of chips in front of him. I had a smaller stack of chips. We'd already been playing for several hours. He, unlike myself, had to work in the morning.

"What do you want to do?" the tournament director asked.

"How about play one hand and whoever wins gets all the money?" I suggested.

"Um, no," Jacob said.

He added, "We could chop, though."

"Chop" meant split up the winnings. The number-three finisher had left in a huff after a bad hand, so there were extra stakes.

"Okay," I said. "How about we stop now, you take $70, and I get $30 and the gift card?"

He thought about it for a second and extended his hand.

And thus I began my march toward free chicken-wing poker glory.

Two nights later, I returned to Fowler's on karaoke Thursday. The woman who ran the stage usually played poker from seven to nine, went bust, and then set up the karaoke machine and walked around offering $3 electric-blue Jell-O shots. I wanted to be at the card table with the people pounding the Jell-O shots, because soon they'd get sloppy and stagger out to the patio for a smoke and a dangerous drive home. Karaoke and cars led to odd scenes, like the strangely sexy woman who enjoyed getting wasted and singing "Hotel California" on a wireless mike while also playing a hand, or the disgusting slob with mustard on his collar who would get up and suddenly belt out a pitch-perfect Tony Bennett cover.

Singing karaoke earned 5,000 chips per song. I've enjoyed singing in public, so I always signed up for two songs. The karaoke list was extensive, but the patrons seemed to like '90s hip-hop and horrible bro-country songs the best. I do best in low registers, so I tended to stick to two Johnny Cash standards: "Ring of Fire" and "Understand Your Man." It became a habit of mine. I would lose, sing "Ring of Fire" around 9:30 p.m., then go home to watch the Dodgers game on delay.

One night, I sauntered into Fowler's with a lot of chips behind me. I gave my second-place $25 gift card to a barback who was also kind of a poker hustler. God knows I didn't want to cash that in for food. I would eat the chicken wings at Fowler's if I had to, but I was trying to keep my figure and also live to see age sixty.

"Thanks for dinner," he said.

He slid me 35,000 in chips, probably more than he should have. Plus, I signed up for my usual two karaoke songs. So that was 45,000 in bonus chips, plus my usual starting stack of 18,000, plus another 5,000 for my merchandise, plus an extra fiver for arriving on time. In the poker world, I was born on third base and thought I'd hit a triple. It was going to take a lot to bust me.

I rolled through that night as untouched as an Ohio State halfback in the season opener against Akron. I can't explain how I did it, because I still had no idea how to play poker well. I hadn't studied what a good starting hand was, I didn't understand the concept of "fold equity," and I couldn't play a flush draw. But I had so many chips to start and played so carefully that no one could lay a hand on me.

At the end of the night, it was just me and a guy named Bryce.

"I just started playing recently," I said.

"You played well," he said. "I used to play all the time, but now I don't play so much anymore. I moved too far away."

"Where do you live?"

"Over by the lake."

This was the level of deep conversation I had grown used to in poker-land. Regardless, there I sat, with a massive stack, facing down Bryce's less-massive stack.

"So do you wanna chop?" I said.

"Sure," Bryce said.

"Okay," I said. "How about I get seventy, you get thirty, and you also get the gift card."

"I'll take the thirty," he said. "But you can keep the gift card."

Such a deal!

"Cool," I said. "Plus, I get to be first. For the points."

"No problem."

"This is my first first-place here!" I said.

He reached his hand across the table.

"Congratulations, dude!" he said.

And that's how I won my first poker tournament. Sixty people had entered Thunderdome. One person had left. That person was me. I was the champion until someone took me out.

It was midnight. Fowler's had completely emptied except for two off-shift waitresses grumbling into their post-work beers, three trolls clacking away on video poker in the back, a tired-looking tournament director, and the karaoke lady, who was still chirpingly working the machine on the off chance someone stumbled into Fowler's after-hours with whiskey in their belly and songs in their heart.

"What do you want to sing?" she asked.

"I already did 'Understand Your Man,'" I said. "Think I'm just gonna go home."

"Nope," she said. "Winner has to sing. House rules."

"Well, shit," I said.

"Dude," Bryce said. "You gotta sing. You gotta celebrate. This is your first win!"

"Okay," I said. "Let's do 'Hot for Teacher.'"

She fired it up; unfortunately for me, it was much faster and cheesier than I remembered it, and at a much higher pitch than I could handle. So I staggered through it tunelessly, though I did deliver "I brought my pennn-cil" with a lot of horny energy. Still, it was a moment of great triumph. Bryce grabbed an inflatable guitar and air-wailed through the Eddie Van Halen guitar solos, leaning back and tongue wagging, as the video-poker machines chink-chinked deep into the Austin night.

NO MORE DEATH

"You have a lot more of an edge than you used to," Regina said, as I stumbled stoned around the kitchen late in the afternoon, grousing and looking for snacks.

"So?" I said.

"Just an observation."

"Maybe I do," I said, looking at her heartlessly. "*And I like it.*"

Later, she said, "That was the most chilling thing I've ever heard you say."

We'd been grieving for a long time. In January 2016, more than a year before my dad went into the hospital and my mom suddenly died, we lost Hercules. Regina and I adopted Hercules from a breeder in Western Pennsylvania—we were living in Philadelphia at the time—in the fall of 2001, more than a year before our son was born. Hercules was our first baby, and we treated him like one. He rarely barked and couldn't swim. We had to carry him over puddles. He licked our legs neurotically, sometimes so relentlessly that we had to move him away. In his later years, he took to lying on my yoga mat while I practiced in my office. We loved him so.

Though he'd been healthy for most of his life, Herky had been declining for a couple of years. His vision faded, and so did his hearing. We had to leave him overnight at the vet a couple of times.

"He doesn't have much longer," I said to Regina.

"You don't know that," she said.

But I did.

We let Herky sleep in bed with us pretty much every night, to the detriment of our noses and the cleanliness of our sheets. One night, he was acting pretty restless, burrowing and pacing in the covers. Regina and I wanted to get some sleep, so I picked him up and put him in the living room.

When I got up to get some coffee eight hours later, Hercules was in the kitchen, turning around frantically in a small circle. He'd splattered the tile with liquid feces and blood. I immediately picked him up and put him outside, where he exploded again.

"You'd better come out here now," I called to Regina.

She saw the wreckage.

"Oh my God," she said.

Just the day before, I'd been sitting on the couch with a friend. Hercules had jumped up on me, wearing his adorable little doggy diaper, and let me rub his belly. He'd wriggled around in ecstasy and had given me lots of nice little kisses.

It turned out he was saying goodbye.

Regina picked up our suffering dog and rocked him in a chair. His face calmed down. It almost looked like he was smiling. But soon enough, he started panting again. We got into the car and drove him to the emergency vet clinic down the street. But it was too late. As we sat there, Hercules died in Regina's arms.

When I met Regina, she had two cats, and I had two cats. We'd adopted two dogs since we'd been together. Now the whole lot was dead.

"No more pets for a while, okay?" I said.

She agreed, but she also said, "Someday, we're going to replace him."

Within a few months, Regina began to plot. She found a Boston terrier breeder outside of Corpus Christi, followed her Facebook page, and began corresponding. She'd call me into the living room to watch videos of puppies romping around, or adult dogs splashing in an inflatable pool. It was like she had imaginary dog friends just a few hours away.

"You want one," she said. "You know you do."

"Maybe," I said.

But then my mom died, and I'd had enough of death. If we got a dog, that dog would die. What was the point?

In the summer, our house resembled a dorm. Our teenager slept until noon or beyond, and often he didn't sleep at home at all. Regina was also out of school. It was a good time to get a puppy. Mom had been gone for two months when Regina announced that the breeder had one for us.

"How much is it going to cost?" I asked.

She told me.

"That's a lot," I said.

"Come on," she said. "Puppy!"

Jumping up and down, she squealed, "Puppy! Puppy! Puppy!"

She wanted to replace Hercules. I wasn't ready. But I also wasn't exactly in touch with my feelings that summer.

"Fine," I said.

Little dog toys started arriving in the mail. Regina bought food bowls. One afternoon, she called me over to her computer to have me look at dog collars.

"Which design do you like?" she asked.

"I don't like any of them," I said.

"Come on," she said. "It's for the puppy."

"I don't want a puppy."

"Sure you do."

"My mom *died*," I said. "Hercules *died*."

"So you need something new to love."

"No, *you* need something new to love."

"What are you saying?"

"I'm saying I don't want a dog! But you do, I know. It's all about you."

I stood up, throwing my arms around, voice raised and snide. I was very stoned. That was the norm. What ensued doesn't make me look very good. But it happened.

"'I want a dog, me, me, me!'" I said, sneering. "My dog! Good dog! Good little doggy!"

And now I was making my wife cry.

"My whole life, I've had a pet," she said. "I have to have an animal to love."

"You just want a pet so you can love something instead of loving me," I said.

"That's not true."

"NO FUCKING DOG!" I said. "Do you understand? NO MORE DEATH!"

The next day, Regina contacted the breeder and canceled our dog order. There would be no little friend for her on the long nights when I went out to do lord knows what. And the longer I stayed away, the more she got used to life without me. Our teenage son already had one foot out of the nest. A dog represented a domestic anchor, the holy symbol of our life together, a life that grew more precarious every time I played a hand or smoked a joint. I grabbed my stash of weed and headed out to the chicken-wing bar.

"I'm going to play poker," I said, slamming the door behind me.

● ● ●

I went to play a Texas Hold'em tournament in a private house, co-hosted by a guy who sold me weed sometimes. Everyone there had their own stash. I went on an enormous heater and blew out several players more experienced than me. This got me to the final table. Seated next to the host, I noticed he was holding down his cards with a little metal facsimile of the Death Star.

"I like that," I said.

He opened it up to reveal some dank shake.

"It's a grinder," he said.

Then I smoked some hash.

I looked down at my cards, in early position. An ace-nine of spades, a decent speculative hand, but nothing to lose my shit over. I took a big breath and prepared for my heroic moment.

"I'm all in," I said.

The next three people folded. Then a guy said, "I'm also all in."

Great. The table folded around to our host, who said, reluctantly, "I'm gonna call," and flipped over a pair of kings. The other guy had ace-king. They destroyed me, and I blew away my stack. Too stoned to drive, I went into the other room, where the other losers were playing laconically at the kitchen table for pennies.

"That was a bold move," my drug dealer said to me later, and by *bold* he meant *dumb*.

It was both bold *and* dumb. And it wouldn't be my last.

THERE'S NO CRYING IN BASEBALL

The Dodgers had a great season the year my mother died. The two things didn't have anything to do with each other, except in my mind. But it all went down at the same time. I used baseball to deal with my broken heart.

On the Friday after Mom's funeral, my high school friend Jason took me to a spring-training game in Glendale, which made for a cheery night of me saying "I'm okay, really I am," while it felt like a beehive had been cracked open in my body. Two days later, I ended my shift monitoring Dad in the hospital, snuck away to Tempe Diablo Stadium to watch the Dodgers play the Angels, and nobly made it back to the hospital in time for the evening shift. Baseball was the opposite of grief, especially when my team embarked on a 105-win season and an epic World Series run. As the season progressed, I soaked my troubles in a bath of vaporizer hits, statistics, and come-from-behind wins. In a time of great trouble, the Dodgers were my balm and my salvation. Until they weren't.

In mid-October, I went to my twenty-fifth college reunion in Chicago. The playoffs were ongoing, and the Dodgers were in the midst of easily dispatching the Diamondbacks in a three-game sweep on their way to destiny. On the plane back home, I sat next to an attractive blonde woman who looked about twenty years younger than me. I hesitate to use her real name, but let's call her Amanda.

"Are you a fan?" she asked.

I was very high on a marijuana gummy bear that I'd taken before flying, so it didn't quite register.

"Excuse me?" I said.

"Are you a Dodger fan, or do you just like the hat?"

"Oh, I'm a fan," I said.

I still remembered the last time they'd won it all, in 1988. Then, I'd been a college freshman in Chicago, where basically no one else cared about the Dodgers, living in an artsy residence hall, where basically no one else cared about baseball. I watched Game One of the Series alone in my dorm lounge on a flickering 17-inch TV. When Kirk Gibson hit the homer to win Game One, I ran around the stairwell in my pajamas, whooping and slapping walls, bothering everyone who was doing important college stuff like studying and listening to records and making out.

So I was used to meeting indifference when it came to my love of the Dodgers. I had some friends from my disastrous years in LA who were fans, but people in LA only cared casually about anything. Even though I grew up in Phoenix and never even went to a game at the Stadium until I was in my twenties, Vin Scully narrated my childhood as the kindly baseball grandpa I never had. I remembered 1977 and 1978 and 1981. But I especially remembered '88. I knew what victory felt like, and I longed to share that feeling with someone who cared as much as I did.

As it turned out, Amanda was a fan, too, and not just a fan. A *superfan*. In fact, I'd never met anyone outside of a beat reporter who knew as much about the Dodgers as she did. We spiraled down a deep hole of Dodgers ephemera. We knew all about Kiké Hernández's minor-league history, and about Clayton Kershaw's charity work in Africa, and Joc Pederson's special relationship with his little brother, Champ. She knew all about Dodger history, too, going back to the Mike Piazza era at least, and could even remember that disastrous season when Jim Tracy started Jason Phillips at first base. Here, at last, I'd found my ultimate baseball buddy, and she lived in Austin.

"We should watch a game together," I said.

"For sure," she said.

"Let's swap numbers."

"Absolutely."

"It's just about baseball," I said. "I'm married."

"I'm married, too," she said.

There you go. It was just about baseball. I got home and told my wife excitedly about the attractive young blonde Dodgers fan I met on the airplane.

"We're going to watch a game together and it will be awesome and her husband will be there!" I said, as I took a hork off my vape.

"Who is this woman again?" Regina asked.

The playoffs continued. In the National League Championship Series, the Dodgers drew the Cubs and won the first game. Then they won the second game. Amanda and I texted:

"LMK if you are having a watch party Tuesday. It is a great moment in Dodger history," I wrote.

"OMG!!!!!!" she wrote.

"This is what it felt like in 1988," I wrote, followed by "Dre!" when Andre Ethier got a hit.

"My man!" she typed back.

"My bobblehead just gained value."

Looking back on the texts now, there were a lot more of my texts than there were of hers. Mine were detailed descriptions of game actions, where hers were just short phrases like "I knew it" or "Banana Power!!!!"

I started to look at third-party ticket sites. Prices were soaring for potential World Series seats. The Dodgers would be hosting the first two games in LA and decisions had to be made. After the Dodgers won a third game, I cashed in all my frequent flier miles on Delta, even though Series tickets were now retailing at $1,400 a pop. Then I contacted my sister and said, "I'm coming to town for the World Series and I'm going to stay with you." No options were given.

I wrote to Amanda: "I have my plane ticket. Leaving Sunday a.m., gonna pray for a miracle."

"Believe," she wrote back.

Meanwhile, my wife said to me, "You are going to LA but you don't have a ticket?"

"I have to go," I said. "The Dodgers are going to be in the World Series. This means everything to me."

"Is that woman going to be there?" she said.

Regina had every right to be concerned. She indulged my baseball mania, but she wasn't a "fan" in the same way. I'd been erratic since my mother had died. Any kind of behavior was on the table.

"I have no idea," I said. "This isn't about that. It's about baseball. This could be the greatest thing that's ever happened to me."

"You need to be good," said Regina.

"Oh, I'll be good," I said. "The Dodgers are going to be in the World Series!"

What could possibly go wrong?

● ● ●

Game One was on a Tuesday. I got into town on Sunday morning and spent the day hanging out with my beloved nieces, since of course I would be too busy later. My sister gave me my niece Katie's room and that night I dreamed of the World Series as my feet hung off the edge of a pink lace-frilled blanket. The perky visage of YouTuber Joey Graceffa, Katie's favorite, gazed upon me as I surfed ticket sites and obsessively played hand after hand of online poker.

Monday dawned, beginning a week of self-indulgence that would prove excessive even by my standards. The World Series was coming, and with it, unparalleled adventure. I slept in until eleven and then did some yoga while my sister's pet poodle watched me skeptically. I was definitely a real man doing pushups in a room full of Harry Potter books and *Tiger Beat* photos. When I was done, I paced the house nervously, scarfing down an entire bag of Stacy's Pita Chips. The time had come for me to buy some drugs.

California voters had recently legalized recreational marijuana, but it wasn't quite for sale in stores yet. I wasn't going to let that stop me, though. I'd gone online and found a list of weed shops that were bucking the law and selling to anyone before it was legal. One of them was in Van Nuys, not too far from where my sister and her family lived. I drove over.

The shop was in a dark corner of a seedy strip mall just off Van Nuys Boulevard. I parked in a tight spot and went up to the mirrored door, where a security guard poked his head out.

"What's up?" he said.

"I'm here to buy some weed," I said.

"Can I see your ID?" he said.

I showed it to him.

"You're from Texas."

"Unfortunately, yes."

"We can't sell to you unless you're from California and have a medical card."

My card had expired years before.

"But I thought it was legal," I said.

"Come back in two weeks."

My timing was terrible. But weed always finds a way. I leaned against the gray stucco façade, trying to look casual, figuring out my mark. After a few minutes, a woman walked toward the dispensary with purpose. She wore a sleeveless shirt advertising a boxing gym and had an athletic bag thrown over a tatted shoulder. There was no way, I figured, that someone like this, who seemed totally healthy, would deny a fellow stoner his medicine.

"Excuse me?" I said.

She looked up at the bearded white dude wearing a Dodgers cap and a T-shirt that read "Mr. Jackpots," an obscure *Twin Peaks* reference, and didn't blink. This was LA after all. A lot of guys looked like that.

"What?" she said.

"I'm from out of town and I thought recreational was legal, but it turns out that it'll be a couple of weeks."

I flashed her my Texas ID.

"Why are you wearing a Dodgers hat if you're from Texas?"

"It's a long story," I said. "Anyway, if I give you twenty bucks, will you bring me the fattest pre-roll you can find in there? I prefer sativa."

She looked me over, sighed, and held out her hand.

"Fine," she said. "It'll be about five minutes."

"No problem," I said.

Seven minutes passed. I twitched restlessly. She emerged with a fatty enclosed in a plastic tube, plus eight dollars in change.

"This is my favorite pre-roll," she said. "It's a hybrid."

"I don't know," I said. "Too much indica makes me crazy sometimes."

"You won't have any trouble with this one," she said. "I love it."

I should have been wary. What works for a tough-ass boxer from Van Nuys might not work so well for a grieving middle-aged Jew with compulsion issues. In the car, I took the joint out of its plastic tube, and then looked up a review of the brand online. They covered their pre-rolls with kief, little shiny crystals of highly concentrated THC. This was less like a blunt and more like a hit off the crack pipe. One hit and I'd be higher than Snoop backstage.

But I abstained for the moment.

I had to go play some poker.

• • •

I'd been plotting a visit to the casino at Commerce, a legendary LA sleaze-pit where I'd played occasionally when I lived there. But now I was ready to return with thousands of pages of book-learning, a four-figure bankroll, and many hands under my belt. Sure, it was the site of the California State Poker Championships, but that didn't scare me. After winning a tournament at Fowler's chicken-wing bar, I was ready to prowl with what I considered the big cats, but what were actually the low minor leagues.

Commerce holds two tournaments a day, for a modest $60 entry fee. I had ten twenties in my wallet and I was ready to walk out with at least double that, maybe even triple. When someone told my life story in *Rolled: How One Man Used Grief to Propel Him to All-Time Poker Glory*, this would be a key plot point, the moment when I rose up and the poker world began to take notice. I was ready.

In fact, I was so ready that I got to the casino two hours ahead of game time. I got my Commerce player ID card made. Looking at the photo now, my beard was so thick that it would have made Mandy Patinkin envious. After that process ended, I still had an hour and forty-five minutes left. I was tempted by the fatty back in my vehicle, but I resisted. I wanted to be sober and sharp for the five-hour tournament. So instead I did my old routine: I dined at the casino.

From my LA days a decade earlier, I had fond memories of eating at the tables. If you flagged down a waiter, they'd bring you a heaping plate of fried rice so you could chow down hard during the dead times. Fried rice would fill my belly but not too much. It would be my karma food. So I went to the restaurant at the casino—which was even dingier than I remembered, a nightmare of torn leather and photos of faded boxers and second-rate quarterbacks—and ordered up a platter of disgusting stir-fry and a plus-sized Diet Coke, and reviewed hand charts on my phone. What an ace I was! Just like the Dodgers, I would cruise to victory.

The tournament began at six sharp on a raised platform away from the main floor. One player tried to bluff me with a pair of sevens, but I read his face correctly and took a bunch of his chips. Another pot went to me with trip 10s. I was drawing solid cards, observing the table correctly. In particular, I had my eye on a guy down the table, who looked like a young Elliott Gould in *California Split*. He played very conservatively and was clearly no one I wanted to tangle with.

I picked up an ace-queen suited and raised to three times the big blind. Everyone folded but Elliott Gould, who flat-called me. A queen came on the flop, so I bet large. He doubled me and I doubled him. He called. From there, it was all checking on the turn and the river. He turned over a pair of aces. I was in trouble.

Yet at the one-hour mark, I was still in the game. Going all-in on an ace–king paid off when an ace and a king showed up on the flop. Pocket nines won me a small pot, too. Then I looked down and saw my pair of aces, in pocket. Elliot Gould had beaten me with pocket rockets, and now I would clear the field. I bet huge, five times the big blind. Only the guy directly to my left called. The flop came 5, 5, jack.

"All in," I said.

"Call," he said, immediately, and I knew I was dead.

He flipped over an ace–five, suited.

"Shoulda gone all-in preflop," I said.

Elliott Gould shrugged. My aces had been broken. Poker, as it liked to do, had discarded me like yesterday's catch.

"Screw it," I said. I stood up from the table, went to the gift shop, and bought a Snickers bar for energy.

I was going to win back that money.

After a quick pace around the casino, I put myself on the list for the only game for which I was truly qualified: The $40 maximum buy-in, $1–$2 cash tables, the poker equivalent of sandlot ball. I got seated within a few minutes, handed my forty bucks to the dealer, and proceeded to play tighter than Ebenezer Scrooge on payday. No one was going to get more than a single bet out of me. It was like squeezing a drop of juice out of a dry lemon. I was determined to not lose my initial $40 buy-in, and to win back the sixty I'd paid out to get cracked in the tournament.

Guys—or at least mostly guys—came and went from the table, many of them reeking of weed. My joint sat in the car, but I wasn't flying on anything stronger than Diet Coke. I went up ten bucks and down ten bucks, hour after hour, not budging unless I had something decent. The cards fell and fell and I didn't get much. At 11:00 p.m., I could see the tournament breaking up, winners finally declared. I kept grinding, but the profit didn't come. I felt exhausted and sweaty, but the thought of going home and collapsing into my niece's baby bed didn't really appeal to me. There were dollars yet to win.

"What are you doing?" said a woman to my left, who was making a habit of risking all her coins on jack–four off suit because she was "feeling lucky." "All you do is raise and fold, raise and fold."

Clearly, this woman hadn't read *Doyle Brunson's Super System*. She hadn't studied the Doug Polk article, "How to Crush Low Stakes Cash Games Like a Boss." I felt deeply indignant. Maybe playing poker for seven hours straight wasn't so good for my psyche, or maybe my psyche wasn't well suited for playing poker in the first place.

"How DARE you talk to me like that?" I said. "You don't know me! You don't know my game! You can't criticize my playing! I know exactly what I'm doing."

"Jeez, I was just joking," she said.

"There's no joking in poker," I said.

These people weren't my friends.

I was *working*.

Finally, at 2:00 a.m., I drew a pair of pocket kings. A king came out on the flop, and a couple of drunk guys threw all their chips into the middle for no particular reason. I made the call, raked in an $85 pot, and saw my stack, tall and thick, in front of my face.

"See, I told you all, you have to be patient," I said. "It's a matter of timing, of knowing when . . ."

"You talk too much," said the dealer.

A few hands later, I went up to the cashier's window. My total haul for the night was 111 dollars. I'd played poker for more than eight hours, including a full tournament, and had returned a solid eleven-dollar profit. It wasn't much, but it also wasn't a loss.

I had taken my revenge at Commerce.

The clock had already turned.

It was time for the World Series.

● ● ●

After a short and restless night where I dreamt mostly of cards, I got out of my niece's bed, choked down two Diet Cokes, and drove to Eagle Rock to hang out with an old LA yoga friend. While the rest of the world worked and worried and ground through their miserable days worrying about Donald Trump, I was on a self-styled improvised baseball holiday. The first game would be that night, but I didn't have tickets and didn't really plan to get them. Prices were over $1,000 on the resale sites. I was texting with a friend and he said, "I wouldn't pay more than $100 to go into Dodger Stadium, even for the Series. That place is a shithole."

True enough, but I still wanted to be close to the Stadium, to feel the aura, to know success and happiness. And I had a power joint. As soon as I got to my friend's house, I sparked it up, though she wasn't interested in partaking. I smoked about a third of it before I realized that I couldn't feel my fingers. The temperature outside approached 100 degrees. I was stoned and roasting in Southern California and life was good.

Amanda texted me.

"In Echo Park with my dad!"

"Really?" I texted back. "Are you going to the game?"

"Still looking for tix!"

I wanted to celebrate with my fellow Dodgers fans. My yoga friend was very kind and sweet, but she would only be interested in the Dodgers game if there was a free harmonium session and Zen meditation afterward. I needed baseball support.

"I'm right next door," I wrote. "I'll meet ya at least to say hi! Where are you guys?"

"We are heading to our Airbnb here shortly then off to the Short Stop."

The Short Stop was a legendary dive in the shadows of the Stadium where you could drink crummy beer and meet the worst people in the world. I hated going there. But I loved the idea of meeting my friend there and celebrating the greatest moment in baseball history. I took another long drag off my crack joint.

"You going to the game?" she wrote.

I hadn't been planning on it; my intention had been to hit Game Two. But suddenly, my plans were changing.

"It is so hot!!!" I typed.

"Yeah hoping to buy tickets from someone who has them with that thought!" she said.

Pause.

"I am interested," I typed. "Do you need a ride?"

"Walking to Short Stop, we are .2 miles so we don't need a ride."

"Okay I am nearby," I said.

"Cool," she typed.

I put down my joint, turned to my friend, and said,

"I gotta go."

"Why?" she said.

"Well, I met this chick on the plane and she's going down to the World Series and I'm just going to meet up with her before the game to celebrate."

My friend looked at me quizzically.

"Does Regina know about this?"

"Ha ha," I said sarcastically. "It's fine. This woman is with her dad!"

"Still."

"It's fine," I said.

"Are you okay to drive?"

"Oh, sure."

I wheeled down to Echo Park in no time, high as balls, and found a free parking spot in the neighborhood south of the Stadium. The game wouldn't start for five hours, so anyone who planned to attend Game One of the World Series was either still taking meetings or waiting in traffic on the 105 or calling around saying "Hey, I have a World Series ticket" because fewer people give a crap about the Dodgers than one might think. I walked down the hill to the Short Stop and whatever glorious destiny awaited me.

The bar stank of farts and fan sweat. A DJ played hype music off in the corner and a wall of thick-shouldered men, wearing gear, hopped around.

"Let's go Dodgers!" they yelled. "Fuck the Astros!"

Fuck the Astros? I thought. Fuck the *Yankees*, sure, and fuck the Giants to hell, but the Astros weren't a natural rival, just a small impediment to glory.

"Hey!" I heard.

I turned around and saw Amanda, looking fresh and cute and young in a Dodgers half shirt. She gave me a big hug, and I realized that I had made a huge mistake. It didn't matter that I was married and that she was married. This still made no logical sense. We weren't actually friends. This was an uncomfortable situation made real by poor judgment.

"Happy World Series!" I said.

"I know, right?" she said.

Lurking behind her was an older guy with a walrus mustache and a very suspicious look on his face.

"This is my dad," she said.

I shook his hand.

"Pleasure to meet you, sir," I said. "It's a glorious day!"

And I'm very high right now.

"Dad, this is the guy from the plane," she said.

"What guy from what plane?" he said.

He and I made conversation for a while. Apparently, his fandom went back to Brooklyn. He'd enjoyed a career in the Marines and the CIA. He seemed about as interested in talking to me as he would to a random weirdo at the grocery store.

My friend from the plane was looking at third-party ticket sites on her phone.

"How are the prices?" I asked.

"Still pretty high," she said.

"Well," I said. "I'm here! If they go down, maybe I'll join you . . ."

Did I have the money for a World Series ticket? Not really. But I felt the fever. It would be the first World Series game in Dodger Stadium in nearly thirty years. What better way to enjoy it than with my random young female friend who I'd never seen outside of the airplane, and with her dad who hated me?

Maybe the weed was clouding my judgment.

Her dad motioned her away. I stood off to the side while he dragged her into a photo booth and I could see her face fill with shame as he wagged his finger in her face. His upper lip twitched as he shook with rage. I wish I could have heard what he said, but it was probably something like,

"So you decided to invite a married man to come along with us to the World Series. Did you tell your husband about this? What the hell is wrong with you? I raised you better than this. You have brought shame upon our family and the Dodgers and the entire world."

She returned looking like she'd just been grounded.

"So listen, this is supposed to just be a father-daughter thing, and . . ." she said.

"No worries," I said.

Her father appeared next to her. I shook his hand.

"Have a nice time!" I said.

I backed out the door.

"Go Blue!"

So instead of going to the game, I drove over to my friends' apartment and watched it on a small TV while their eight-year-old played games on the iPad, occasionally asking, "What is that man who's throwing the ball called?" Outside, during the commercial breaks, I smoked three kinds of weed, including my never-ending crack joint.

"I know what those do," my friend said. "I'm not touching that shit."

I thought I was fine. It was a great game, the Dodgers won, but I felt strange. Even though I hadn't done anything particularly wrong, I'd done something *terribly* wrong. If I had any integrity left, I'd just betrayed it terribly to chase . . . I didn't even know what I was chasing, or maybe I did. Either way, it wasn't healthy. A curse had been placed upon me and upon all of baseball. Regardless, I thought, I'd just hit Game Two. I hadn't flown all the way to California for nothing.

● ● ●

I didn't get a lot of sleep that night. My brain felt beyond twitchy. It seemed to exist on another plane.

Addiction literature talks about going "into the bubble," where all that matters is satisfying your urge, scratching your itch, retreating into fantasy to avoid difficult emotion. My bubble floated way above the earth, like a blimp advertising my dysfunction. In my fantasy, the World Series had been created solely for me, to remove all my grief and anxiety. The drugs were an extra float in my nonstop fun parade.

As soon as I woke up, I began monitoring ticket sites. I'd been looking at them on and off all night. I saw a few tickets hovering around $850, but those were in the upper deck, with bad sightlines. Anything in the loge, my preferred game location, was well into the $1,200 range. I didn't have that kind of money. What was I doing here? What was I trying to prove?

Then, around ten thirty, a "deal" popped up, a field level box seat, down the right field line, for just under $900. I called my wife.

"I found a ticket to the game," I said.

"How much is it?" she said.

I told her.

"No way," she said.

"I'm thinking about it."

"How are you going to pay for it?"

"We have room on the Visa."

"How are you going to pay the Visa bill?"

"Look," I said, "it's been a terrible year for me. The Dodgers are all I have."

"You have me," she said. "And your son."

"You guys aren't in the World Series. Come on, I've always wanted to go to a World Series game. I flew all the way here."

"That is a lot of money."

"Regina . . . *My mom died.*"

"You had better figure out a way to pay off that ticket," she said. "This is your birthday and your Christmas gift forever."

I hung up and bought a $900 ticket to a baseball game. The bubble had inflated to five times its normal size. I floated high above the earth, living in a baseball fantasy.

"Screw it, I bought a ticket. I have always wanted to go to a World Series game and now I will! #worldseries," I posted on Facebook and Instagram and Twitter, when really I should have kept it all to myself.

Gates opened at 2:00 p.m. I only had three hours to get to the game. I was going to have to leave soon. A couple days earlier, I'd gotten a message from a random "friend" on Facebook who I'd never met. After heavily advertising that I was in LA, I'd left myself open for messages like, "If you're around Echo Park I'd love to meet up, smoke a bowl or whatever," the key phrase being *smoke a bowl*.

I'd rarely been to Dodger Stadium when I wasn't completely baked out of my wits, and the World Series hardly seemed like a time to start. Also, he said he "admired" my writing, serving up free food for my hungry ego.

As soon as I posted that I'd bought a ticket, the random guy messaged me.

"You around?" he said.

"Yeah," I said. "But I am headed for the Stadium!"

"Ha ha," he said. "Game is not for four hours."

The specter of *free marijuana* loomed.

"Is your place w/in walking distance?" I typed.

"Yes," he said. "I mean, it is about a half mile to the park."

"That is pretty close," I said.

"I watched the jets fly over my house."

Street parking, he said, was available for free.

"GET ME STONED BRO," I typed.

"I'm on a hill," he warned.

And so, on one of the biggest days of my life, when I'd shelled out nearly a grand for a single baseball ticket, instead of going to the Stadium, I drove to some random address on Lucretia Avenue where a random guy awaited me with bags of weed. You might call that poor judgment.

Most people wouldn't go over to some strange guy's house based off a random invitation, even if that strange guy liked their writing. But I was a trusting soul with an enormous ego. Plus I liked drugs, and was willing to put everything at risk to get them. So at around one in the afternoon on the day of Game Two of the 2017 World Series, I pulled up in front of this dude's apartment building in Echo Park.

This guy meant me no harm and he did me no harm. All damage that day was self-inflicted, though the nice variety of pot on his coffee table certainly didn't help my judgment. Before I availed myself of his stash, though, I horked the rest of my kief-flecked super-joint, which had me flying higher than Harrison Ford on a joyride over Malibu Canyon.

My host said he did a ton of power yoga and had the beefy arms to back up that claim. Until recently, he'd been the campaign manager of a favored LA City Council candidate whose campaign collapsed after his bigoted comments about transgender, overweight, and Mexican people were discovered. Needless to say, my host lost his job. He was also going through a divorce and was currently involved in a sexual "triad" with two younger women he'd met at a bar.

"That sure sounds healthy," I said, horking a big bowl of weed.

"They're into it," he said. "Besides, it's only temporary because I'm moving to Indonesia in the fall."

The conversation was juicy and the weed was good. I wasn't disappointed with my choice, except that I looked at my phone. It was 3:15 p.m., the World Series game started in two hours, and I was so high that I could barely stand up.

"I better get going," I said. "How far away is the Stadium again?"

"It's not too far," he said. "But you're going to have to walk some hills."

Walking hills shouldn't have been a problem, since I was in at least average shape for a forty-seven-year-old stoner. But it was nearly 100 degrees that day and I didn't have a bottle of water. Plus, a half mile isn't a straight shot in Echo Park, and it was twenty minutes before I saw a single fellow fan walking the streets. Car after car cruised past me as I wandered around side streets that never saw baseball traffic. I finally turned into Elysian Park and marched straight upward into the ravine. I must have walked for forty-five minutes directly upward. By the time I reached the parking lot entrance, my Vin Scully "It's Time for Dodger Baseball" shirt was completely soaked in sweat. Little sweat globules hung off my beard hairs. Now I was stoned, exhausted, *and* dehydrated. But I still had an hour and half until game time.

Grinning like a little boy at the zoo, I approached the gate, ticket in hand. I handed it to the guy. He scanned it. His scanner gun beeped.

"This ticket has already been used," he said.

"WHAT?" I said.

"It was scanned at 2:03 p.m."

He crossed his arms arrogantly.

"But that can't be," I said. "I bought it. It's not true."

He scanned it again.

"Sir," he said. "You're going to have to back away."

As I always do in a crisis, I handled this situation calmly and rationally. I wagged my finger in his face.

"How *dare* you tell me to back away?" I said. "I've waited my entire life for this. It's not possible. This can't be happening. I paid NINE HUNDRED DOLLARS FOR THIS TICKET!"

"That is not my problem," he said.

"Is there a supervisor I can talk to?"

"Wait over there," he said.

He got on a radio.

A hard-ass-looking guy in a black suit approached.

"How can I help you, sir?" he said.

"Your guy says my ticket's no good!" I said. "But that isn't possible. I bought it!"

"Where did you buy it, sir? At the Stadium?"

"No, I bought it from . . ."

"You need to take this up with the ticket seller," he said.

"But . . ." I said. "It was a legitimate third-party site?"

"Ticket scalping is illegal."

"Are you fucking kidding me?" I said. "Half the people here are using scalped tickets."

"Not as far as I know, sir. You will have to call the people you bought the ticket from."

"But . . ."

He stood there with his arms crossed.

"Please step away from the gate, sir."

And then I realized:

I wasn't going to the World Series after all.

The guy stood there with his arms crossed, next to the ticket scanner, who also had his arms crossed. Here I was, an innocent Dodger fan out to have the time of his life, and instead, I was being treated like a criminal by the team that I'd loved from boyhood. This wasn't right. This wasn't fair. I *deserved* to be happy.

I walked away and squatted next to a garbage can.

"FUCK!!!!" I screamed, as loudly as I could.

I looked up. A phalanx of employees, literally wearing brown shirts, was closing ranks around me. The supervisor stood at the front of them, arms crossed.

"Sir," he said.

"But . . ." I said.

"We're going to have to ask you to leave the gate."

"I . . . I just wanted to go to the World Series," I said.

"That is not my problem, sir. Please leave."

I was full of rage and self-pity. Everything had gone wrong. And if I did or said one more thing, I imagined, I was going to spend Game Two of the World Series handcuffed to a chair in the basement of Dodger Stadium. If I hadn't been a white guy, even a pathetic-looking white guy like me, I almost certainly would have gone to jail.

I turned around and moped toward the parking lot.

After a few hundred feet, I reached a souvenir stand.

"Can I help you, sir?" the kid behind the table asked.

I dropped to my knees and began to sob.

"I just wanted to go to the World Series and they won't let me in!" I said. "Why? Why are they doing this to me?"

"You should probably talk to customer relations," said the kid.

"*MY MOTHER DIED!*" I cried.

He didn't respond. I crawled away. After I wrenched myself up on the bumper of a pickup truck, I approached a guy who was wandering around the parking lot. I showed him my ticket.

"This looks legit, right?"

"Where did you buy it?" he said.

I told him.

"And the Stadium security wouldn't let me in," I said, sobbing. "They were so *mean!*"

He shrugged his shoulders and walked away. In the mirror of the pickup truck, I saw a sweaty old man with snot in his graying beard, his tear-filled eyes bloodshot from drug abuse. That man was me. Mom wouldn't have been proud.

For the next hour, I wandered outside the many entrances of Dodger Stadium, up and down the levels, crying like a toddler, desperate for someone who could solve my problem. Each person I talked to in the parking lot or the ticket window or even at the door to the clubhouse was more dismissive and unkinder than the next.

"I can't believe they're treating me like this," I said to a guy who was waiting in line.

"That's LA for you," he said.

"Well fuck LA," I said. *"AND FUCK THE DODGERS!"* I shouted.

Parents who were taking their kids to the World Series moved them away from me, the crazy man in the parking lot. *No wait,* I wanted to say. *I'm just like them. Just a little boy who wants to go to a baseball game.*

It all could have ended if just one person had taken a second to kindly explain to me that I needed to call the third-party ticket company. Instead, all I got was obfuscation. Then it occurred to me: all the talk about how the Dodgers were a family organization that integrated baseball and saved generations of Americans from prejudice, all that stuff about the "Dodger tradition"—it was just nostalgic PR nonsense. The Dodgers were a cold, heartless hedge fund that didn't care about its fans or their boyhood memories. We weren't customers. We were just numbers through the turnstiles. I don't know why I'd never realized that before. A forty-year-bubble popped, and I wouldn't be able to see the team the same way ever again. While I behaved like an entitled and wasted shit, I'll never forget the cold-hearted cruelty I encountered that day. I'd given my life and my heart to that stupid baseball team, and they treated me like a criminal.

Naturally, I was all over social media in a panic about my "situation." My friend Jerod called me, making fun of me, saying, "You're acting like you're a refugee or something.

"Neal," he said. "Just call the ticket company. They'll make good."

So I did that. I got a nice woman on the phone. Instead of saying, "Hey, I bought a ticket from you all and it didn't scan at the entrance," I said, "I always dreamed of going to the World Series (*sniff*), but I got here and they wouldn't let me in (*snuffle*), and they were so mean to me and I walked all over and they almost arrested me and they treated me like a criminal!"

"Oh boy," she said.

Then I really poured it on.

"My mom died this year and it was always her dream to go to a baseball game with me!"

This was a lie. My mom hated baseball. Maybe it was her dream to see Carlos Montoya play flamenco guitar at Carnegie Hall, but she didn't give one whit about the World Series.

"Why were they so mean to me?" I cried.

"Oh, honey," the ticket woman said. "I don't know. People are like that sometimes."

And so it came to pass that I weaseled my way into her giving me an amazing seat in the loge section behind home plate, a premium seat at any price. I slid into my World Series seat just as the National Anthem was ending and got to see the Dodgers take the lead early, knock out Justin Verlander, blow that lead in the ninth inning, and choke away the game in extras. It was a legendary World Series game with a horrifying ending for Dodgers fans.

At the airport on the way back home, I was in line for coffee. I saw Amanda. She and the old man had tickets on my return flight home.

"Oh hi," she said, and walked away without looking back.

Truly a friendship to last a lifetime.

PART TWO:

SOBER

OUT OF THE FOG

There were basically no consequences for my completely reckless two-day drugs-and-gambling binge. All that happened was that I went to a World Series game and racked up a big credit card debt that I was able to pay off within a few months. But inside, something had changed.

I felt shaky for a week afterward. My memory of the World Series would always be tainted by the fact that I'd behaved without integrity, on that day and in many more facets of my life. It was enough. The Dodgers may have lost the World Series, but I'd won something more important: my sobriety.

For two days, I lay in bed, sweating. My muscles ached and I had a bad headache. But then it felt over. I didn't have to go to rehab; I didn't even have to go see my general practitioner. It felt less like wrenching myself away from a chemical dependency and more like breaking a bad habit. A really bad one. Marijuana is certainly addictive, but I've had tougher detoxes from barbecued brisket or particularly bad sessions of cards. I've jonesed harder for seltzer on a hot day than I did for marijuana back in November of 2017.

Still, I felt like I'd been in some dark club all night. The doors flung open, the hazy sun shone right into my eyes as I staggered forward out of the fog, looking for coffee. I'd spent twenty-five years getting high, and now I wasn't getting high any more. Everything just seemed so *weird*. Could I see clearly now? The weed had gone.

But what exactly did getting sober even mean? I wasn't sure. For the first time in years, maybe even decades, I wasn't getting stoned before dinner, or before doing the dishes. I stopped getting high before watching TV, including *Jeopardy!*. It was hard to gauge if my recall had become sharper, because I was spending most of my time saying, "I'm not high right now. That is so weird."

When was the last time I'd done *anything* sober? During my stoned years, whole episodes of TV shows had floated by me without me remembering them. I'd played videos on YouTube over and over again because I thought they were awesome, but they weren't awesome. I almost never caught the important plot twists in tricky movies, or even in simple ones. Sometimes, entire character arcs would pass by without me noticing them. I suppose that happened to me in real life as well.

When you're stoned, you have to do *everything* stoned. *The Amazing Race* is going to be on soon, I'd thought. Time to get high. Have you ever watched *The Amazing Race?* It's not a stoner show. I've since watched it quite a few times, not high. And I've still kind of enjoyed it, though maybe not as much. It's hard to tell. I don't remember.

Regina looked shocked when I told her how many drugs I'd been doing. "I had no idea it was that bad," she said. She really didn't. When she left the house, I got high, often outside so she wouldn't smell the weed. I got high in the middle of the night sometimes. If I ran out, I'd smoke resin. I'd vape a nug in my Silver Surfer until it looked like coal. Sometimes my diet reduced down to nothing but lighter fluid and ash.

Here I was, not stoned. But that's very different than sober. I'd taken a couple of months off back in 2013, too, but no one could seriously say I'd achieved physical or emotional sobriety. I'd still only thought of myself, of my needs, of my awesomeness. I looked like a middle-aged man but acted and thought like a teenager. What did getting sober even mean? I had no idea.

• • •

The Infiniti corporation emailed, offering me a car junket to Los Angeles, the chance to drive some dumb, meaningless compact sports-utility vehicle model in the midst of its "mid-cycle refresh."

"I think I'm gonna take the trip," I said to Regina.

"Do you think that's a good idea?" she said.

It had been all of six weeks since I'd stopped getting high. I'd been nicer, kinder, more pleasant, more willing to help. Regina seemed awfully pleased at the new reality developing. But she also understood that it was shaky, and that a trip to LA, the scene of my last major pot crime and a place where marijuana was now available in stores for real, might not be such a good idea.

But the addict way of thinking still held. I needed to get out of town for a while. No, I *deserved* to get out of town.

"I'll be fine," I said.

• • •

I drove all day in the hills around Malibu. The car had "the world's first variable rate compression engine," according to the press kit, though I still don't know what that means and I don't care. All I know is that my drive partner wanted to take some photos and video of the car with the beach as the backdrop, which would have been a huge waste of three hours for me. So instead, I got to drive a different car back to the hotel, in West Hollywood, by myself.

Suddenly, I found myself alone in Los Angeles, completely unsupervised, with many hours before I had a commitment and at least sixty bucks in my pocket. Before I'd left town, I'd done a map search and I could see that there were three dispensaries within a mile. All of them walking distance. But I was in even *better* shape, because I had a car. And no one was monitoring where it was and when I had to return it.

Well, I thought. I could just swing by the dispensary and get myself a little pack of Cheeba Chews. That would only be twenty bucks, no one would ever know, and I could have a nice little party watching TV and eating room service.

No, I said to myself.

Maybe just one cartridge and a disposable vape pen? Or a mellow pre-rolled joint?

Naughty boy.

Okay, okay, I thought. What about just going to a dispensary and buying a twenty-four-ounce CBD-only soda? CBD doesn't get you high. It just relaxes you, all body effects and none of the mental effects. My real addiction wasn't to cannabis, anyway. It was to THC!

Of course, I understood that if I stepped foot in a dispensary for five minutes, I'd be as helpless as a sailor without earplugs headed into the realm of the sirens. There's no way I'd be able to resist the call of the cannabis. I'd chase that CBD soda with a special Rice Krispies treat and then I'd head back to the dispensary for more.

My palms were wet on the steering wheel. My breath grew shallow. It was relatively easy to shut down my weed connections in Texas; I just had to erase a couple of numbers from my phone. They didn't sell it in stores. In LA, buying weed was easier than buying batteries.

I needed help.

Back at the hotel, I got into the tub. I filled it with warm water first. Then I went on my phone and Googled "marijuana addiction Los Angeles." It was 4:00 p.m. The water got cold after thirty minutes. Then I watched a movie, *Wind River*, starring Jeremy Renner and Elizabeth Olsen, two minor Avengers battling evil oil-field workers in rural Alaska. That was sure depressing, but it took my mind off my cravings.

At 7:00 p.m., I had a dinner thing with the drive program. I left early. The driver dropped me off in front a twelve-step center in West Hollywood. Then, on a Friday night at eight thirty, I went to a Marijuana Anonymous meeting. It wasn't my first. I'd been to a few in Austin in the preceding weeks. But this was the biggest: the World Series of Marijuana Anonymous meetings, as it were.

Since then, I've learned that twelve-step meetings operate under a principle of attraction, not promotion. Members retain complete anonymity at all levels of media. Unless they choose to write memoirs and articles and do podcasts about themselves. Here I am, open about my addiction, unashamed if not completely proud. But everyone else I've met along the way will remain in obscurity.

That said, the room was packed with people, some of whom had years of sobriety, others who confessed that they were stoned at *that very moment*. One woman said, "I'm trying to find some hobbies, but getting high *is* my hobby." After the meeting, I went out to a dumpy Hollywood diner, not high, with a bunch of strangers. They all talked about how marijuana had led them to make some really bad sexual choices. At that point, I realized that being sober wasn't going to be any less weird than being on drugs all the time.

"My name is Neal," I said at the meeting. "And I'm a pothead."

I'd found my people, or at least some of them. The level of honesty I heard at that meeting kind of amazed me, and it made me realize that I needed to reach that level, too. If I wanted to get sober, I was going to have to do a lot more than not smoke weed; I was going to have to take a long, hard look at myself. It wouldn't be fun. Then again, I'd had plenty of fun in my life. Look where that had gotten me.

POWERLESS

When I was in Texas, I had to buy my dope from dealers. For a while I went to a guy's apartment across town. He and I were both quite passionate about legalization and we'd talk excitedly about the end of Prohibition while he rooted around in his closets and under his couches to find his stash. Then we'd smoke a couple of bowls before I handed him sixty bucks. One time he informed me he had a couple of cold sores, but I got high with him anyway. These were the risks you had to take.

At some point, my dealer stopped returning my calls. I grew desperate, and found myself rooting around at the bottom of a shoebox where I kept my paraphernalia, digging up leaf fragments from three-year-old plastic bags, scraping pipes with a paper clip, and puffing on ash, just to get a little hit. Finally, he called and asked me to meet him in a supermarket parking lot more or less on my side of town.

I drove over there and got into his beater. He was wearing nicer clothes than usual. "I'm trying to sell to higher-volume clients," he told me. No more $50–$60 eighths for him. He was moving up the food chain. There were other dealers in town who dealt with small potatoes like me. He said he'd put me in touch with them, but he never did.

As I left that car with my little bag of weed, I'd never felt like more of a drug addict. Until two weeks later, when I was sitting in a friend's apartment waiting for his roommate, who I'd entrusted with another sixty bucks, to come through the door with some goodies from a "secret dispensary" that had opened up in town. Or a month after that, when I went over to some dude's house and he pulled the cover off an unused hot tub, revealing enough kind bud to keep Willie Nelson's tour bus high for a year.

In this environment, I entered recovery. Like a lot of people who come into the Twelve Steps cold, I found the jargon annoying—the talk about daily prayer and meditation, "conscious contact" with a higher power, and "character flaws and defects." Yet beneath all the blah-blah recovery talk is a powerful formula for self-improvement.

In Step One, you have to admit you're powerless over your addiction. To me, that means coming to terms with the fact that you actually *are* an addict, and that the addiction has fundamentally messed up your life. In front of my group, I gave a shortened version of this book, essentially a confession of my sins.

Then come some "God Steps." You have to turn the care of your life to a higher power. Though my parents raised me Jewish, I don't believe in the Jewish God as he's written. It never resonated with me. As Jon Stewart once said, I remained Jewish because of all the delicious snacks. But I did have my yoga practice. I'd lain in *savasana*—corpse pose— and felt the energy of the universe coursing through my body.

I had known and sensed the presence of something greater and more transcendent than myself. So a higher power was never too far away from my mind.

I did a worksheet in which I delineated my many character flaws and defects: my ego, my insecurities, my resentments, my disappointments, my destructive sexual thoughts and behaviors. And I made a list of people I resented and how my negative qualities manifested in those resentments. Basically, I took a long, hard look at myself, and found myself wanting.

Then I made a list of people I'd wronged in my addiction. In the case of people not deeply connected to my life every day, I sent some uncomfortable emails and made some awkward phone calls. In the case of my wife and son, I tried to do what the programs call a "living amends," to improve the way I treat them on a daily basis. I cooked dinner more. I did more chores. When my son was home sick from school, I grumbled less and cared for him more.

Once I straightened out my shit a little, I also started sponsoring other guys in the program. For a certain kind of aimless urban artsy hipster, I'm a good model of sobriety, I suppose. When they called or emailed with a problem, I answered, usually sympathetically. But if they showed signs of weakness, I put down the hammer. If I wasn't going to get to smoke pot, *they* weren't going to get to smoke pot.

Basically, I just started living my life with more dignity and integrity, with intermittent success. The days of me rooting around my Willie Nelson-brand grinder with a paper clip to root out any unsmoked particles of kief ended at last. My Silver Surfer vaporizer, which had been a centerpiece of my desk for so long, got moved to the closet. I gave away all remaining gummy bears and tossed random bags of schwag into the garbage. Marijuana, which had been the linchpin of my emotional, social, and mental life for so many years, became something that I used to do, like tubing down the Salt

River or voluntarily going to poetry readings. Gradually, as the haze began to burn off my brain, I began to piece together the wreck. But I also kept playing poker.

THE PROBLEM WITH POKER

Three weeks into recovery, I went back to the stoner poker game. This time would be different, though. I would be sober. Everyone else would be so baked that I was going to clobber them. I'd just bide my time and then around 10:00 p.m., when they were wasted beyond belief, I'd strike.

"I'm gonna play," I told Regina.

"Do you think this is a good idea?" Regina asked.

"I think it's an *excellent* idea," I said.

"Okay, dear," she said, still patiently waiting for me to ride out this phase.

I went to the poker night. As before, everyone had their own stash. They passed the pipes and joints and little dabs of hash around the table in a circle. Maybe I got a contact high, but I didn't get an actual high. I felt clearheaded. But the stacks were low, so one bad move meant death. My ace got outkicked. Someone drew out a straight on my pocket pair. Even though I was the only sober guy in the bunch, my chips disappeared within an hour.

Then I sat at the kitchen table—the "losers' table"; I peeled three twenty-dollar bills off my bankroll and waited for the other losers to join me. Most of them were stoned to the gills. I was determined to win back my $80 buy-in and vowed to stay all night until that happened. My vow proved prophetic. Hour after hour I sat at that table in that dank, smoky room, waiting to press my advantage. Every time the pipe came around, I passed it along. By 2:00 a.m., it was just me and three red-eyed die-hards sitting around the table. I scooped an $80 pot, the game ended, and I cashed out. By the final count, I came out two dollars ahead. I wasn't a loser, no sir.

 • • •

The Texas Fantasy Poker League held a tournament a few times a year called Poker Palooza. It was free to enter. The winner got and continues to get a round-trip ticket to Vegas, four nights in a hotel room, and a $1,000 entry to a World Series of Poker event. My game had improved. I'd been studying quite a bit, and had built up a $3,000 bankroll. In my mind, I'd become quite a poker player.

When you're new in recovery and trying to stem compulsive behavior, maybe it's not a good idea to enter a multi-hundred-person poker tournament. But I was determined.

"Are you sure this is a good idea?" said Regina, in what was becoming a common refrain.

"Eh, it's free," I said. "What harm could it do?"

The tournament was scheduled to start at 11:00 a.m.

"I probably won't win," I said to Regina.

"You almost definitely won't," she said.

"Right," I said. "So I should be back by two. Or three. Four at the latest."

"Fine," she said. "Have fun."

I went to a local grocery store and bought a $20 gift card for the league to donate to charity. This won me a few thousand extra chips, which I was going to need to survive.

This Poker Palooza took place at a vintage arcade and fun center called Pinballz. Conveniently located two miles from my house, Pinballz featured hundreds of arcade games, Skee-Ball, air hockey, laser tag, decent bar food, and a fully stocked liquor cabinet. The event room in the back was all red brick and plastic tables, like a low-rent union hall. The ceilings were low, and the back doors emptied onto Dumpster Alley. It made a small-town VFW on a Monday night seem glamorous. I took my bag of poker chips and my 32-ounce Diet Coke and sat down to clean up against these clowns.

Zack, whose heart clearly wasn't in his Palooza experience, bombed out within half an hour. He'd recently purchased a ping-pong table, so his obsessions had shifted. I was playing a lot stronger. Within a couple of hours, I'd doubled my stack. By the second break, the contestants had been cut in half. Tables were starting to consolidate. I could see my way to the finals. Soon, I'd be traveling to Las Vegas where I would take my place among poker royalty.

That's about when the real players started turning up their juice. I got bluffed out of a pot by a woman who'd won the tournament twice before. Even though she had a broken foot and was pretty clearly hopped up on pain pills, she was still a better poker player than I'd ever be. Then a middle-aged Indian guy, who I'd never seen before, sat down. I made idle chitchat with him.

I picked up a pair of aces. He raised. I tripled his bet. Another guy down the line called me, going all-in. The guy folded.

I won the pot when the other guy flipped over a pair of sixes. The Indian guy said, "You play very predictably."

Well, I'd show him! The next time he bet, I went all in with a jack-five suited. He called, flipped over a king-jack, and took all my chips. I walked away from the table, stunned and defeated, and indignant. That trick had worked when I'd seen Doug Polk do it on YouTube! As I stood there shaking my head among the vintage pinball machines, my skin felt prickly. My brain was on fire with cards. My phone read only 2:30 p.m.; I wasn't done with poker yet.

I got into my car, drove to the bank, and withdrew $330 from the special bank account I'd set up to handle my poker winnings.

"Got eliminated," I texted a lie to Regina. "Gonna play another tournament. For free. Be home in a few hours."

What the hell? I thought. It doesn't matter. It's only poker.

In fact, there was no other tournament. I drove the access road, did a quick turnaround, and pulled into the parking lot of the Texas Card House. This was a local gambling den where I'd won and lost large sums of money throughout the summer after my mother died. That water ran *deep* with sharks. But I considered myself one of them. I'd win a few hundred bucks and be home long before dinner. Though Regina wouldn't like me going there, she didn't have to know. I put my phone on airplane mode. A man needs his privacy when he's working.

● ● ●

Five hours later, I was still at the Card House, down $120. My stomach had dropped to the floor. I found myself thinking, "Just one big hand and I'm outta here."

I found myself, just after 8:00 p.m., still at the tables *after* losing the grimiest free poker tournament this side of the Continental Divide; I was about as far away from a Zen state as I could imagine. To make things worse, I was trapped at a table with the worst patron of the Texas Card House, a guy who wore a MAGA hat and an American-flag T-shirt and lapped up pot after pot, exclaiming "It's too easy!" while chugging Coors Light tallboys. Of course, I'd seen other MAGA hats, and had heard all kinds of political opinions at the table. But he threw them out aggressively, embodying the worst qualities of any person, left or right. He set out to intimidate, and I had lost my Zen.

I tossed in my cards to a big bet.

"Folded, like a weak fucking pussy," he said.

"Language, sir," said the dealer, a proper fellow who didn't like the F-word at his table.

"Thank you," I said.

"*Thank you,*" the other player sneered.

I pursed my lips. He leaned toward me.

"Why don't you get on your knees," he whispered. "Purse your lips. Suck that cock."

I smoldered. It was all welling up inside of me, just like it had at Dodger Stadium. Maybe I'd stopped smoking weed, but my "character defects," as they say in the twelve-step meetings, still hadn't been eradicated. To be fair, I was still newly sober, but I'd willfully and recklessly put myself in a situation where I could be exploited. And now it was all going to blow.

"Like the weak little pussy boy you are. Wipe that cum off your lips and . . ."

"*You sonofabitch!*" I shouted. "*You do not talk to me that way!*"

"Hey, easy," he said.

"No, *you take it easy!*" I said. "How *dare you talk to me like that?*"

"Oh boy," said one of my fellow players.

I turned around. A security guard stood behind me. I was within seconds of getting tossed out of a poker club, a place where the threshold for bad behavior is pretty high. The guy sat there with his arms crossed. He didn't have to scoop any more pots. As far as he was concerned, he'd already won.

"Apologize to him," the security guard said.

"I'll try to watch what I say," he said.

"Mmmmph," I said.

By 9:00 p.m., I was completely busted. In the parking lot, I turned on my phone. It contained four voice mails and more than a dozen texts, that were basically, "WHERE ARE YOU??????" Even my normally chill son had called to say, "Dad, Mom is frantically pacing around the house, you need to call her."

When I opened my front door fifteen minutes later, Regina was sitting on the couch, metaphorically chain-smoking.

"What were you doing?" she asked.

"Playing poker," I said.

"I last heard from you SEVEN HOURS AGO? Where were you?"

"The Card House," I said.

"You went to the Card House after losing that tournament," she said.

"Yes."

"I thought you were playing in another tournament," she said.

"I was," I lied. "At the Card House."

"How much money did you lose?" she asked.

"Not much," I lied again.

"YOU CAN'T DO THAT!" she said.

I sat down in a chair and buried my head in my hands.

"I'm sorry," I said. "I think I might have a problem. I'm really sorry. So sorry. I should not have turned off my phone. Sorry. Sorry. Sorry."

"Stop groveling," she said.

"Sorry," I said.

"You need to stop playing poker. You *have to stop.*"

"But I still have a decent bankroll," I said. "I can get this under control. I promise. Today was bad, but I can pull it together."

"Straighten up, Pollack," she said. "This isn't about you losing money. It's about your commitments. To me. To your son. To everything."

• • •

Dad had gotten sick again. I'd only been sober for a few weeks. Since my mom died, he'd almost fully recovered, spending the summer hiking in Colorado with his sister, looking slimmer and healthier than he had in years. Then he returned to Arizona, to an empty house, and couldn't keep up the routine. His life had become a slog of procedures and tests.

On January 2, I got a call from my sister.

"Dad was having chest pains," she said. "I just wanted to let you know. He called an ambulance."

"This is it," I said to Regina.

"You've said that before," she said.

A couple hours later, my sister texted me.

"He ate a bunch of pickled pigs' feet," she said. "These are digestion issues."

We all had a good laugh about that. At last, my dad's appetite for old country snacks had come back to get him. The laughter ended the next morning. I woke up to this text:

"Gallstones. One is stuck. Tomorrow a.m. has to have an endoscopy to remove it. Not surgery. I will make sure he is comfortable tonight and come back in the a.m."

He'd been admitted to the hospital for "pain control." "Lots of morphine," Rebecca said. They offered him Oxycontin but "we said no to that crazy shit."

The next day, they still hadn't removed the gallstones. He needed to see a cardiologist and a kidney doctor.

"He just asked for morphine for pain," Rebecca said. "I don't know that he was in pain. I think he likes it."

"That is bad," I wrote back. "Morphine is heroin."

"He threw up . . . this is a mess. Sigh."

A CT and an MRI loomed. Meanwhile, he had elevated white blood cells and his blood sugar had spiked to more than 500. After way too many tests they decided that the gallbladder needed to come out.

On January 5, his seventy-fifth birthday, my widowed dad had his gallbladder removed. This pretty much defined a bad year. I asked where we should send flowers. But instead, my sisters and I decided that I'd send myself. On the evening on January 8, I flew to Phoenix. Dad was still in the hospital. I'd go see him in the morning. Feeling stressed and anxious, my addict needed to turn somewhere for a fix.

I'd found a poker app.

On April 15, 2011, or, as it's known in the poker world, "Black Friday," the online poker world in the United States effectively shut down. Those who'd made a huge living fishing for suckers online suddenly found vast bankrolls up to seven figures confiscated by the feds. The party ended. And yet over the years, it had gradually built back up. New apps emerged. You could still play if you lived in New Jersey or Nevada. And nothing in the laws prevented anyone, from any state, from playing online poker if the client originated in a foreign country.

Initially, I just played the free tournaments on an app run out of Panama called BetOnline. But these, I soon realized, were taking up six hours of my day. I could easily piss away four hours in pursuit of a ten-dollar cash-out, passing it off as "work," and then lose, and before I knew it, it was 2:00 p.m. and I was still sitting in bed in my underwear. So I decided to pursue what I considered a more productive line.

I'd taken $25 of my bankroll and socked it into BetOnline. It took about a month of playing penny-ante games, but eventually BetOnline took all $25. Then I plowed another $100 into the site. This would be, I said, my final investment.

Online poker moves about thirty times faster than regular poker. And you can play as many tables as you can handle at one time. For months, I just ground it out at one table, focusing as tightly as I could, trying to ignore the trolls in the chat. My moniker on the site was "Doctorbenway," pretentiously named after a William Burroughs character in *Naked Lunch*.

It wasn't real life.

By the time I got to Phoenix, I'd become a multi-tabler. I had the BetOnline app on my laptop, and I often found myself playing two tables at a time. Sometimes three. I'd even have a couple of cash games open while piling into a tournament at the same time. I learned to identify good situations and bad situations immediately. On a given day, I could run thousands of hand simulations, like a supercomputer. And I actually started making money. At one point, I got the account up to $250, not easy to do in the penny-ante games.

I got online at the Austin airport, playing as much as I could. As soon as I got to my dad's house, where I was staying by myself until I picked him up from the hospital, I fired up the app, playing several hands at a time while I plowed through whatever was still edible in his fridge, drinking seltzers from Costco at the dining room table. At around 11:00 p.m., I yawned and stretched and went into the bathroom, keeping the app running while I took a piss and brushed my teeth. Then I got into bed and said, "Just one more tournament." I didn't have to be at the hospital until 10:00 a.m. I closed the app at three o'clock and was up again at seven to play a few more games. The cards blinked across my eyelids when I slept, calling me home for just a few hundred more hands.

I got to the hospital. Dad didn't look so great. He seemed frustrated and exhausted and he really just wanted to go home. We had a nice fifteen-minute conversation, which was about all we had in us, and then he fell asleep. This was the same building where my mother had died less than a year before.

I hooked onto the Wi-Fi and immediately started playing the Zynga Poker app. I really needed anything I could to distract me. By the end of the day, Dad still hadn't been cleared to go home so I went back to the house, walked his dog, and immediately got back onto my computer to play more poker.

I drove him home the next day and did my best to play formerly stoned butler. He was asleep in bed within minutes, granting me the opportunity to get on the computer and play poker for another six hours or so. I managed to get him to his chair and fixed him a little food, and after that was done and he had *NCIS* playing on the TV, I returned to the app. It went like that for three days. I slept maybe four hours a night, because I found a new kind of tournament where half the players cashed in if they could conspire to eliminate the other half. This would ultimately prove my downfall on BetOnline. But I started winning. When I won, I always deluded myself into thinking that I'd never lose again.

Dad had started to feel better by the time I left. I'd started to feel worse. At this point, I was burning through up to eight screens at a time. Cards fluttered past my eyelids like the big board changing arrival times and destinations at Penn Station. My synapses had been shredded. I was within a step of losing contact with reality entirely. I started googling *Is online poker addictive?* As if I didn't already know the answer.

My flight home was delayed by two hours. That time went by fast because the airport had free Wi-Fi. When I got home, Regina said to me,

"I don't understand why you're so tired."

"It was stressful taking care of my dad," I said, as I squirreled away to my office to play a couple of tournaments.

At 3:00 a.m., I got out of bed, flipped open the laptop, and opened a few windows. Forty-five minutes later, Regina appeared at the doorway in her bathrobe.

"JUST A SECOND!" I shouted.

"You need to delete that damn poker app now."

"But I'm up $175!" I said.

"I don't care."

"But—"

"Stop. Playing. Poker."

"I'll cash out," I promised.

Four days later, all that money was gone. I didn't cash out, but I did delete the app. Then, during a mishap where I dropped a bag of potting soil while attempting to help Regina with a plant while simultaneously doing a tournament, I deleted Zynga Poker as well.

It was time to start cleaning up my mess.

SOBER TENT

I'd been sober for nearly a year. Elijah was just about to turn sixteen. We'd become business partners of sorts. We co-wrote articles together and he contributed reviews to a pop-culture site that I was editing. He hacked out pieces about a *Family Guy* coffee table book, the HBO shows *Euphoria* and *Game of Thrones*, and the Spanish crime soap opera, *Money Heist*. Typing at home without a shirt on was the family business.

We persuaded an editor to send us to the Austin City Limits Festival in 2018. I had about as much interest in ACL as I had in getting a colonoscopy, but Elijah was extremely excited, so I agreed to co-write an article.

Elijah had a blast. Meanwhile, I glumly sat with some friends who got super stoned while watching the Wombats, a rock group from Liverpool who were perfectly fine but sounded like Oasis had gone through the copying machine from *Multiplicity* a few times. Then it was time for the Breeders, who filled the crowd with nostalgia but left me feeling dead inside, which is really just the inverse of nostalgia.

Everyone around me was getting high, but I wasn't getting high. Maybe I'd only enjoyed seeing live music in the first place *because* I was high, but I certainly wasn't enjoying it now. It was possible that the live music I was seeing was just bad. I'd discovered that other activities I enjoyed, like yoga, or hiking, or cooking, or reading, or simply watching TV, were perfectly enjoyable without marijuana. But the music left me feeling deader than the discarded cans of White Claw Hard Seltzer that I saw sprinkling the yellowed lawn of Zilker Park. What was wrong with me?

While everyone around me horked joints and vape pens, I drank warm water, trying not to die. I wandered away from the Breeders. Nearby was a sign:

"Sober Tent."

This was just what I needed! First of all, it was a tent, which meant it provided shade. People were at a table, passing out literature.

"I'm sober," I said.

"Good for you, man," they said.

A guy who used to be a Deadhead had started the Sober Tent phenomenon for people who still wanted to go to music festivals without getting wasted. I wasn't particularly sure I still wanted to go to music festivals, but I *was* interested in staying sober.

"We're having a meeting at four thirty," he said.

And so it came to pass that I found myself under the Sober Tent on a hot Saturday afternoon, in a circle with twenty other people, all of whom were alcoholics, or drug addicts, or sex addicts, or food addicts, or codependents, or some combination thereof, plus other addictions of which they were either aware or unaware. Regardless, we all said the Serenity Prayer together while a guy dressed as a giant pickle watched us from outside the tent, giving us a thumbs-up.

God, grant me the serenity to accept the things I cannot change,

Courage to change the things I can,

And wisdom to know the difference.

Then we began passing around a large yellow balloon. At old-school Dead shows, people—who called themselves "Wharf Rats"—carried yellow balloons to indicate their sobriety. Now I was one of them, I guessed.

People confessed their sins and talked about how fucked up they used to get at shows. About halfway through the circle, the yellow balloon came to me.

"Hi, I'm Neal, and I'm a pothead," I said.

"Hi Neal!"

"So, this is my first time at a music festival without getting high," I said. "And I have to admit that I'm pretty bored!"

I wasn't exactly having fun in the Sober Tent, but it's always nice to know that there are other people out there as miserable as I am. Still, I left the meeting feeling pretty good, and blessed to finally be free of drugs.

● ● ●

On Monday, after Elijah went to school, I got a big garbage bag and went to the shelf in my office where I kept all my drug paraphernalia. I still had dozens of pipes and packages of Zig-Zag papers and pens and other weed ephemera that I'd collected over the years. I scooped it all into the bag—all the tea tins, the shoeboxes full of glass, the dugouts and one-hitters. Away went my grinders and my vapes and my pipe cleaners and Ziploc bags and discarded edible wrappers. Finally, with a sigh, I took my beloved Silver Surfer and pitched it into the bag as well. I'd been sober for nearly a year. It was time. Also, I didn't need the temptation. I pitched it all into the trash, and now it's at some dump somewhere, never to be smoked or vaped again.

When Elijah got home from school, I asked him to come into my office.

"What?" he said, annoyed with me as usual.

"I want to show you something," I said.

"What is it?" he said. "I'm kinda busy."

I handed him some of the little plastic disks I'd been accumulating at the meetings.

"These indicate various lengths of sobriety," I said.

"They're pretty cheap-looking," he said.

"Yep," I said. "I'm getting my one-year chip next month."

"Wow," he said. "Have you really been sober for a year?"

I was sober, and my son was well aware. Maybe I still had a chance as a dad.

THE DREAM
DOG APPEARS

My life had improved. There were no more public meltdowns. There were no more *private* meltdowns. I exercised more, cooked more, read more, went for long walks, and actually focused on what people were saying when they talked to me. For the first time in years, and possibly ever, I was a present and active participant in my own life. I was no longer playing a role, or a persona. Sometimes my days would feel shaky, but I owned them.

Throughout everything, I kept practicing yoga. It would be a literal stretch to say that yoga helped me get sober. After all, I spent years vaping on the mat while playacting mindfulness. I even *taught* yoga stoned.

And it's hard to say if my practice improved or changed after I quit the weed. For years, I'd been paying eighteen dollars a month for a website embarrassingly called YogaGlo. Now they've changed the name to just Glo, which is even worse. But the teachers on YogaGlo included my guru Richard Freeman, as well as dozens of other top instructors from all over the world. Classes ranged greatly in difficulty and in length. You could do active yoga or passive, restorative yoga. If I had stiff hips, or needed to de-stress from traveling, YogaGlo offered targeted videos. There was meditation and pranayama and lectures on Buddhist principles.

YogaGlo had two teachers who were openly in recovery—one of them, Elena Brower, from marijuana. They offered individual classes and also a full course in Yoga for Recovery. I did all of them, multiple times. The classes were easy and gentle, with a focus on grounding and breath. Anything I'd done or said or thought in the past could stay in the past. In in the present moment, everything was fine. Basically, this was the message I'd heard in every decent yoga class since I'd started practicing fifteen years earlier. But I was finally ready to hear it. Even if that message came on a website called Glo.

● ● ●

Regina had been flirting with a dog breeder on Facebook again. The breeder made Boston terriers, which we'd long ago determined was the only dog for us. A dog became available and unlike the last time, I didn't put up any resistance. We made an appointment to go get her. But the breeder pulled out of the agreement because the dog was too hyper and would have been better off on a farm.

Then another dog, Briar, became available. The breeder loved Briar, but Briar always fought with her husband's favorite dog. So the breeder had to give her up, with much sadness. First, though, Briar was pregnant. She needed to have the litter and nurse and then she needed to get spayed. These are the sorts of dramas that occur when you're dealing with a breeder.

Regina began to dog-nest. Hercules's old dog beds reappeared and then got tossed in the washer. Little Amazon packages containing dog toys and collars and treats began to appear at the doorstep.

A few weeks later, Briar was ready. But then the breeder's mom's horse died and they had to bury the horse, so it was delayed again.

"Briar's never going to be here," Regina said.

These also are the sorts of dramas that happen with dog breeders.

On a Saturday morning in June, Regina and I drove south. Because of my weird side job reviewing cars, I had a diesel Ford F-150 Lariat edition truck that week, so we blended right into rural Texas. We drove it through the South-Central Texas barbecue belt, but we didn't stop for meat. That's how excited we were to get a dog.

"It's happening!" Regina said.

Two and a half hours from home, we pulled into a thirty-acre farm somewhere near Corpus Christi. Out of a double-wide trailer burst Briar and her very handsome son, Lord Queso von Taco.

Inside the trailer, the tearful breeder gave us Briar's AKC registration paperwork and all her immunization records. Briar now belonged to us, and the only cost was a modest donation to a charity called the "Smushed Face Rescue Society."

Briar snuggled up to me, and then flopped on her back. She had a very sweet face and enormous saggy nipples. That'll happen when you bear three litters in five years. She and Queso swarmed all over me, and gradually the breeder let other Bostons out of the back where they enveloped me, slurping my face.

We got into the truck. Briar snuggled in next to us, like she would every day for the next seven to nine years. Regina and I improvised a song.

Her name was Briar

She was a show dog

She had her ears up in the air

And her nipples down to there . . .

It had been a dark time in my life, the darkest, but now I was ready to let some light peep through the cracks. Mom was gone. Hercules was gone. But everyone else besides David Bowie was still here. I had my wife, I had my son, I had my dog. My life could be full of love and joy if I'd just let it in, and if I never did drugs ever again.

We pulled away from the ranch, the truck leaving a thick cloud of dust wafting behind. The dog settled between us, her back paw on my leg and her head in Regina's lap. That dog was going to bring us tons of kisses and friendship. My social-media feed was about to become nothing but Briar pictures. She would quickly become the legend of my life. Regina looked happy. For once, finally, her happiness was all that mattered.

"Look at this beautiful girl," she said.

"Let's take her home," I said.

● ● ●

Years ago, my imaginary arch-enemy Andrew Sullivan, a writer I'd been making fun of for years, wrote an essay about coming out of the "cannabis closet." He considered himself very brave for revealing to the world that he was a stoner. I thought he was *weak*. I'd been out and proud for a decade by the time Sully started preaching about weed's magical properties.

About a year after I quit, I committed my own act of editorial "bravery." I came out of the marijuana addict's closet, by publishing an editorial in the *New York Times*. "I'm Just a Middle-Aged House Dad Addicted to Pot," went the headline. "My name is Neal, and I'm a marijuana addict," it began.

If you've read this far, the content will be familiar to you. I smoked a lot of weed, I pulled down my pants in public, I got into bar fights while high, and, stricken by unimaginable grief and THC so strong I might as well have been smoking crack, I almost got arrested at Dodger Stadium during the 2017 World Series. Then I talked about how I'd entered recovery and had been clean for almost a year.

And that was it. The public knew. I'd like to say something like, "The response was swift and furious," or, "I received an outpouring of thousands of responses unlike anything I could ever imagine"—but mostly I received some kind, gentle supportive comments from friends. That's pretty much the publicly acceptable way to respond when someone tells you that they're an addict.

It wasn't all positive. There was plenty of "this guy is an idiot," something I'd heard many times before. One dude I went to college with said, "I should be able to drive around with a joint dangling from my lips if I want." *Um, no you shouldn't.*

But the majority of the criticism I received—which, again, was mild and not particularly widespread—could be summed up by people insisting that marijuana isn't addictive. I heard that a lot, from various people, for various reasons. Some of them are concerned that if I "demonize" marijuana as addictive, then that will empower the sinister societal forces that are attempting to keep it illegal. Others are themselves addicted to, or at least codependent on, marijuana, so they're trying to justify their own behavior. I've heard from my share of people who are just libertarian-leaning online trolls. Some people have a passion for marijuana as a wellness solution to everything, and others simply don't believe me.

But the vast majority of the responses I received were from people with whom I'd struck a nerve. I got an email from some random young guy in Wisconsin who was worried that his marijuana habit was hurting his work and making him a less-attentive and less-present dad. I ended up talking to him for an hour on the phone and trying to persuade him to travel to the nearest Marijuana Anonymous meeting fifty miles away from his home. Facebook friends, who were sort of real-life friends, got in touch with me to say that they'd been thinking of quitting themselves, that marijuana had ground their once-vibrant personalities into fine powder, had dulled their brains and poisoned their senses. Email after email came in, from people lost in a fog, unable to quit, snapping awake after years—or even decades—of obsessive marijuana use.

And if they weren't concerned about themselves, they were worried about their spouse, or their boyfriend, or their brother-in-law. I wasn't getting stories about how marijuana had killed people—those don't really exist—but I *was* hearing a lot about how it had *vanished* them.

Again, I don't want to exaggerate. I received a few dozen emails or social-media messages over the course of a year, so didn't exactly have to hire an assistant to deal with them. Hell, I got more responses when I wrote an online piece making fun of Led Zeppelin. But it still made me wonder how deep that iceberg went. I started imagining a country, and a world full of thousands, or even millions, of people, normal-seeming, functioning adults whose lives had either been completely overrun by weed or were getting to that point. In fact, I didn't have to imagine it. I'd lived it, and I knew it was true. And now, I also knew this:

I was not alone.

But what did that mean? I'm still not entirely sure. If I can help some twentysomething just falling under the magical allure of cannabis turn away and live an even more slightly sober life, I'd be happy to do that. I'd also be happy to encourage new parents, who often get high because being a new parent is *stressful,* to quit if the weed is taking over their life. Or maybe I can help give lifelong stoners an excuse to start over, or, possibly, do nothing at all.

I may not have learned much at all these twelve-step meetings I've been attending, and I'm certainly no expert in recovery, but the most important aspect of the meeting lies in something called the Twelve Traditions. These traditions include maintaining total anonymity at all levels of society (unless you choose to, say, write a 250-page recovery memoir); that all twelve-step groups are completely self-supporting and dependent on voluntary contributions; and, most importantly to me, that they promote no particular cause and no particular political point of view. In other words, the most fervent MAGA-hat-wearing Trump supporter should be able to sit down next to a lifelong establishment Democrat at a twelve-step meeting and relate to a common purpose: getting sober. That's certainly played out in my twelve-step experience, where I've found myself sandwiched between soft hippie types and gun-toting, scary ex-Marines. Recovery is the great equalizer.

This especially translates to marijuana addiction. There's not a lot of politics when it comes to alcoholism. Pretty much everyone knows alcohol is dangerous. Millions of people drink anyway. Most people don't judge alcoholics. And Prohibition is a weird historical footnote in Ken Burns documentaries.

With marijuana, the prohibition era, though definitely on a downswing, is still with us. And for many people, the legalization of weed is a primary, if not *the* primary issue. That certainly used to be the case with me. I wouldn't have called myself a single-issue voter, but my main two pet causes—before I sobered up—were marijuana legalization and traffic safety. This made me very fun to sit next to at dinner parties (not that I ever got invited to any of those). I understand why some people got nervous when I published my *New York Times* essay. I was providing cover for marijuana prohibitionists, they said. By providing purely anecdotal evidence of my weird public behavior, without any science to back it up, I was being a useful idiot.

But was I? I'm not particularly interested in the science of addiction, or of marijuana dependency. Even if I were, I have a large gap in my understanding of science, and my trivia statistics bear that out. All I have are my anecdotes and my life experience; they tell me, beyond any doubt, that I was a marijuana addict and that marijuana addiction is real. And since I realized that fact, I've met hundreds of other people who share the same problem.

Politically, that lands me in a somewhat uncomfortable place. On the one hand, I have absolutely no interest in aligning myself with Jeff Sessions, the private-prison complex, small-town Texas sheriff's departments, or the other social forces conspiring to keep marijuana on the black market. Some of these anti-pot warriors are doing it out of public health concerns, but I don't believe that most of them are acting in good faith. Never trust someone who profits from the incarceration of others.

On the other hand, I'm also extremely skeptical of the people who are claiming—and there are a lot of them—that marijuana is some sort of universal miracle wellness cure, and the foundation for all human happiness. It helps some people with some conditions, and then there are CBD-only strains, which is almost like an entirely different drug. But a lot of the marijuana-related wellness and beauty products out there strike me as a particularly dank-smelling form of snake oil. Marijuana is not a health food.

Politically, I've become a sort of marijuana agnostic. I believe it should be legal. No one should be denied a job or an opportunity because one time they got caught smoking or selling weed. Consenting adults should be able to buy it and use it in whatever manner their particular jurisdiction sees fit. If alcohol consumption can be considered an essential human freedom, then so can marijuana.

On the other hand, let's not kid ourselves. Marijuana can be dangerous and addictive. That's the only strong political stand I'll take. The more fully we can acknowledge and admit that as a society, the more we'll be able to help people like me who struggle with overuse, whose lives, in the words of the twelve-step literature, have become unmanageable.

When I published the *Times* piece, I was beginning to manage my own life. I had been sober for nearly a year. Then I got my one-year keychain, and then I went past that year, and beyond. And that was good, because I was going to need all the sobriety I could handle for what came next.

DADDY ISSUES

My father and I had never been friends. At most, for the last fifteen years, we'd established an uneasy détente between us, because I didn't feel like fighting anymore. After he told us that Elijah "wouldn't be my grandson" anymore if we went through with Regina's inclination to not circumcise him, I backed off, mostly for good. Dad grew up in the Bronx and knew how to play mean and dirty.

I'd spent my entire life afraid of my dad's anger. He wasn't tall, but he was thick and fearsome. "Bernard" means "strong as a bear" in German, and he definitely roared like a bear at his worst. His temper could blow up insanely, and out of nowhere. I have an early memory of sitting in a taxi with my little sister while he raged at an airport porter, calling him a *sonofabitch* while a lady outside the taxi said, with decent reason, "Those poor children." More vividly, I recall a time when I put a too-heavy container of detergent on top of a shelf in the laundry room. He chased me around the house, screaming with rage. And then he sat down on the couch, sobbing. This could be forgiven. I've been a dad now, and I know the dumb things children can do. I've been there many times.

From where did all this rage come? My dad's parents met on the boat escaping Germany in 1938. Like many Jews of his generation, he lost a lot of his family in the Holocaust. His father died of cancer when he was eleven. His mother remarried and then that man died soon after, having a heart attack while my father watched. After going to college and participating in the Reserve Officer Training Corps, dad *volunteered* to go to Vietnam. He was among the first wave of soldiers to ship out in 1965. My grandmother, having lost so much already, got depressed, took a big dose of barbiturates, and washed them down with alcohol, while my dad was on the ship to Asia.

My aunt, then a teenager, found my grandmother dead in her bed. She had no way of getting in touch with my father, but she was also getting a lot of pressure from her community to bury her mother. She said she wouldn't do it without her brother's permission. And this is where the story gets strange.

One of my family's neighbors in the apartment building in the Bronx where they lived was a politically connected lawyer named Bob Tofel, who later became my godfather. Somehow, Bob Tofel got in touch with Hubert Humphrey, the Vice President of the United States. Hubert Humphrey sent an emergency telegram to the troop carrier, which was somewhere at sea, to inform my father that his mother had, essentially, committed suicide. My dad sent a telegram to my aunt that said, "Bury her. I'll be home as soon as I can."

As soon as he got home, he took care of family business. And then, even though he had the option to stay stateside because he was the sole support of his sister, he went back. *To Vietnam.* He said he owed something to the United States for rescuing his parents from the Holocaust.

Vietnam, as we all know, didn't go great for any American. So my dad had a lot of reasons to be angry. He often took it out on me.

When I was a teenager, in front of a room full of people, I smarted off to him. Dad struck me in the solar plexus with his flat palm. He'd been in the Army, so he knew exactly where to land the blow. I fell to the ground gasping for air. No one said anything as I writhed around. Dad just went on talking, as though he'd done something good by shutting me down. It didn't leave a mark, and he never did anything like it again. But it sure made me furious at him for most of the rest of my life.

Dad didn't dislike me, and he wasn't ashamed of me. He took a decent amount of pride in my accomplishments, a pride that grew as they became broader and more absurd, if not necessarily more lucrative. When I was sixteen, working on the school newspaper and as a teen correspondent for the afternoon *Phoenix Gazette,* he said to me, "When are you going to stop messing around with that stupid paper and start working for the *New York Times?*" It was an absurdly stupid thing to say to a teenager in 1986. Maybe I was a little sensitive. I stormed away from the dinner table, ran outside, and slammed my car door so hard that I broke the driver's window, and then I had to pay for the new window. Years later, when my byline did appear in the *Times,* he sloughed it off as no big deal.

As an adult, Dad offered me financial advice—which I took sometimes—and sometimes offered me money—which I always took. He also offered his time to help us move, which we did often, and he was very emotionally generous and loving with my son, which I always appreciated.

Sometimes the old conflicts would emerge. One Thanksgiving, when my mom was still alive, Dad decided to get a spiral ham from Costco. He left it on the kitchen counter, covered in a shower cap, so his guests could snack from it.

After two days, the ham started graying. After three days, it turned green. No one went near that ham except my dad, who kept picking at it despite a somewhat sickly odor emanating from under the cap. Finally, I said something.

"Dad, is it a good idea to let people keep eating a ham that color?"

He looked at me, the old rage burning in his eyes. They would have flashed red if they could have. This is what he'd looked like when he'd Hulked out when I was a kid.

"You don't know *shit*," he snarled.

The right thing to do there would be to walk away. But I was high at the time, and I had my patterns. So instead I shouted, "SUCK MY DICK, OLD MAN!" and stormed out of the house. When I lost my temper with Dad, I lost the moral high ground. I was afraid of him, and had been my whole life.

In recovery, and any related therapy, you have to look at the roots of your addiction. It didn't take very far for me to search. My mom had alcoholics on her side of the family, including my grandfather. But on my dad's side of the family, it was all inherited trauma. I can and will blame my marijuana addiction on Adolf Hitler. Why not?

There was nothing dirty or shameful about therapy for my generation. I may not have realized I had an addiction problem, so I wasn't really able to dig down to the roots of and reasons for my many character flaws. But I would have done it if I'd realized I'd had a problem.

My dad, on the other hand, was all denial and reticence. He was smart enough for therapy but didn't have the emotional resources to seek it out, or the intellectual flexibility to realize he might have had a problem. Dad never did drugs, and I don't recall ever seeing him drunk. He poured all his inherited trauma into his temper, and into food. And, in the end, it was the food that killed him.

● ● ●

Dad recovered after my mom died. He came back most of the way. No one exactly ever figured out why his throat had closed up the way it had, though we suspect it may have been from bacteria that came out of a poorly cleaned CPAP machine, which he used to help him with sleep apnea. *That's a very modern problem.*

Regardless, he went to a speech therapist who tried to get him to swallow correctly again. He refused to do his homework, and I don't think he ever got that reflex back entirely. By the time the summer of 2017 arrived, he was well enough to head up to Colorado to stay with his sister. He brought along his dog Cosmo. They walked several miles a day. He ate full home-cooked meals and was surrounded by children and loving family members. Photos from that summer show a smiling old dude with color in his cheeks, looking like he might have a few more years in the tank. Then the summer ended, and that tank started to drain.

Dad went home to Arizona, and without his sister to prop him up, he declined pretty fast. He sat by himself in the big ranch house where he'd raised three children and, with his wife, helped raise six grandchildren, and barely turned on the stove. His diet mostly consisted of blueberry muffins, which he bought in bulk at Costco, and maybe, if he was feeling health-minded, a bowl of cherry tomatoes smothered in sour cream. For a while, he tried to walk the dog, but Cosmo had a lot of energy and needed five fast miles, minimum. After a while, Dad got fed up and started opening the door and letting Cosmo dash out into the desert. When my sisters and I questioned the wisdom of this move, Dad said, "The dog's fine. He always comes home."

The dog was not fine. He ran around the hot streets, tongue wagging. People in the neighborhood picked him up and brought him home. They called the cops, who also picked Cosmo up and brought him home. Eventually, they told my dad that if they caught him letting Cosmo run around again, they'd arrest him. My dad didn't believe them, and just kept letting the dog run around. He didn't have the energy for anything else.

In February of 2018, my sister Rebecca got remarried at a brewery in Scottsdale. Mom would have hated going to a wedding at a brewery in Scottsdale. She was gone of course, but Dad was still here, at least in body.

When Mom was alive, the house was always welcoming, always a party. Not that Dad didn't enjoy some occasional company, but the fiesta was over. The house remained clean and the patio got blown. But now, if something broke, it tended to stay broken. Mom always bugged Dad until he either took care of it himself or called someone in if he couldn't. Now, he didn't have the energy, the attention span, or the will. Rebecca came by once every week or so to water the indoor plants, but they were still dying. Most of the time, three-quarters of the rooms never saw anyone in them at all. The longer Mom was gone, the more the house filled with ghosts.

At the time of the wedding, I wasn't yet three months sober. I'd really only begun to understand what it meant to live free of subservience to my immediate needs and desires, so I was feeling pretty shaky. But I was also starting to feel clear and calm for the first time in many years, maybe ever. I was going to need that calmness.

Dad had agreed to throw a brunch the day after Rebecca's wedding for out-of-town guests. But he didn't really have the energy, and maybe not the budget, to do it up right. He went to Costco and bought a few items—a tray of deli meats, a few snacks, some cookies, and a huge brick of delicious sharp white cheddar cheese. Regina and Elijah and I stayed at the house, and Dad had neglected to buy anything else to eat; the food stores were pretty low. So I took a knife, cut a chunk of cheese, and ate it.

Later, we were in the kitchen. There were guests in from England, and other people around. Dad was going through the food in the fridge and saw that the cheese was no longer intact. His eyes glowed a familiar red.

"You can never keep your hands off the food," he said.

"I was hungry," I said.

"Did you pay for it?"

"Dad, I'm forty-eight years old. I can go buy some more cheese if you want."

He leaned into me.

"You stupid, ungrateful . . ."

In the past, I might have yelled at him. Or I might have pushed him. Or maybe I would have taken the cheese and thrown it on the floor. Instead, I just slinked away.

"I'm sorry I ate the cheese, Dad," I said.

I just felt sad about the whole thing. Here was my only surviving parent, and he was yelling at me because I'd eaten a little cheese before a party. I'm sure he was having all kinds of emotions he couldn't express. Yes, he'd been hurtful, but in the end, it didn't matter. Sobriety had allowed me to see that not everything was about me. The man was suffering, even if he often talked to me like I was garbage.

That night, Dad went to bed early. The wedding was the next day. He was still in bed at noon, his sheets covered in vomit. The night before I'd arrived, he'd gone out with our British "relatives" and eaten liver and onions that didn't agree with him. He could barely move all day. At 3:00 p.m., he staggered out of his bedroom wearing a suit, and made it through the wedding, his eyes distant, his voice shaky.

His health didn't improve from there.

THE HEART
OF THE MATTER

Dad kept letting Cosmo run around the neighborhood. My sister finally stepped in and took the dog away from him.

"Dad, you can't take care of Cosmo anymore," she said, and she was right. Dad finally admitted it.

First, she placed Cosmo with a coworker, who left him sitting outside on the patio all day. Fortunately, it wasn't summer. Cosmo jumped the wall and ended up on someone else's patio. The coworker got fired, for unrelated reasons. Cosmo went back to my dad, who proceeded to unleash him on the neighborhood again.

Desperate, my sisters put up pleas on Facebook and someone answered the call. Miraculously, Cosmo ended up moving onto the vast estate of a former professional hockey player and his family. The last we saw, the family put him on a Christmas card with ribbons in his hair, provided by the two little girls who doted on him. Cosmo got a happy ending. My dad, not so much.

Rebecca came over to the house one day to find my dad sitting in his car in the garage, head resting on the steering wheel. When she asked him how long he'd been like that, he said, "A while." When I talked to him a few days later and asked him how he was, he said, "I'm very weak." Dad would sooner vote for a Democrat than he would admit weakness, so we knew something was seriously wrong with him.

He routinely went to several doctors, all of whom told him different things. There were GPs and specialists, the Mayo Clinic and the VA, doctors to give him pills and give him injections, but no one was manning the ship since my mom died. The doctors did their localized stuff and then Dad went back home to eat his Costco blueberry muffins. He'd been a diabetic for thirty years, so he was constantly having sugar highs and lows and taking his blood and injecting himself and eating mini Snickers bars if he felt faint. Eventually, this routine was going to knock him down.

This time, the cardiologist gave him the real news. He had 90 percent heart blockage, and if he didn't do something about it, he'd be dead within months. As it turns out, he was in stage three kidney failure and had uncontrolled diabetes along with a host of other health problems. He'd be dead within months anyway. But the doctor either didn't know that, didn't care, or, most likely, made a lot of money off performing surgery on desperate old people. He scheduled Dad for quadruple bypass surgery.

Dad survived the surgery. Meanwhile, my sisters and I had been having some difficult conversations. He wasn't cooking for himself anymore; he wasn't doing much of anything, really, other than going to Costco or the occasional Rotary Club meeting. Sometimes he'd talk on the phone with former clients, but he didn't have the energy or the attention span to follow through with anything. He was only seventy-five, but he'd been fading. It was hard to deny that he could no longer take care of himself.

We had a couple of options. We could hire a full-time nurse to move in and take care of him, because someone needed to monitor Dad's food and exercise activity at all times. Just taking his vitals wouldn't be enough. A nurse would be tremendously expensive. No amount of insurance could cover it, and he'd be out of money within a year, maybe two.

The other option involved finding Dad somewhere else to live, another way of saying, "We're putting Father in a home." Rebecca had been looking at places, but Dad didn't seem too interested. Sometimes he told her he'd be willing, other times he told her no way. He'd only be able to afford it if he sold his house, which he'd lived in since 1977.

Regina and Elijah and I flew to Phoenix about a week after Dad's surgery. Whether or not he moved out of the house, we still needed to start culling decades of stuff. I was going to stay in Phoenix with Dad, maybe a week or longer, until he could get steady after the surgery.

Feeling somewhat optimistic, Dad had taken out a lease on a brand-new Toyota RAV4 the week before his quadruple bypass surgery. This lease came with a substantial $425 monthly payment, which seemed like a lot to me for a RAV4. Regardless, it was a new car, and my dad liked it because it had some safety features, which he needed "in case I get tired while I'm driving." I tried to explain to him that cars, even the ones with automatic braking and lane assist, were still at least a decade away from driving themselves, but he just shrugged his shoulders and said, "Ehhhh."

Dad drove his new car a couple of times before he went into the hospital, and never got behind the wheel again. We drove the car to his post-surgery rehab. It was essentially a hospital with weird gilded furniture, a kind of health purgatory for the middle to upper-middle class. You could read the *New York Times* in the computer room. There was physical therapy, and a dining room. It was clean and fairly efficient. I suspected that few people actually left feeling much better than when they came in.

Dad was sitting up in bed, looking pretty rough, but alert. He seemed to have shrunk to half his size. We talked to the nurses and they said he was walking around well, and his vitals seemed strong. The plan was to send him home within thirty-six to forty-eight hours. Regina and Elijah and I went home to prep the house for his arrival.

The next morning, he called me.

"I fell in the dining room," he said.

"Okay," I said.

"I tripped over the chair trying to pull it out."

"And?

"I'm okay," he said.

That was Bernie-speak for "I'm not okay."

When I went to visit him later, the supervisor said they were concerned and that they were going to keep him for another week. Regina and Elijah were driving my mom's old car back to Austin the next day. I was going to be alone in Phoenix in the ghost house where I grew up, waiting to take care of my dad, with whom I rarely got along.

We went in to see him. His arms were bandaged up like a burn victim's. He had a huge bruise on his forehead. He looked like he'd fallen off a horse.

This was definitely going to test my sobriety.

● • ●

Dad's bruises and scabs were healing slowly. In addition, he had some sort of stent in his arm in anticipation of future kidney dialysis, a reality that he continued to reject. The doctor had inserted the stent incorrectly, and his hand and forearm were so puffed up, they looked like a catcher's mitt. His balance was bad. And, let's not forget, he was just getting off quadruple bypass surgery. This was no longer the powerful man who'd made me so afraid when I was a kid.

I went to the rehab center in the late morning, bringing Dad his mail and anything else that had gathered at the house. He wanted to check his email. I asked him if he had Wi-Fi. "I have Safari," he responded. It wasn't worth explaining. We ate lunch together in the dining room. "I wish my son would come have lunch with me," said another one of the old dudes rehabbing at the center, and I realized that the future promised nothing but loneliness and despair.

After lunch we went back to my dad's room. He snoozed in his bed while I nodded off watching the Cubs game, the only available baseball, on WGN. People would come in from time to time to check his vitals or give him dietary advice that he'd ignore.

I tried to make conversation, but after a couple of hours I'd exhausted any last shred of telling him about my modest accomplishments, or Regina's, or Elijah's, or our plans to build a retaining wall in the backyard. Politics were basically off the table lest things take a turn. My mom had always been the one with whom I'd talk about books or movies. And sure, we could talk about food, but Dad was a lot less interested in food than he used to be. So we'd sit, and he'd do the crossword puzzle, or I'd do the crossword puzzle, or he'd nap and I'd look at the little old gray man in the cotton nightie who'd instilled such fear and resentment in me for decades. Finally, it was time for physical therapy or cardiac rehab or whatever, and I'd get bored and leave him.

Then it was back to my boyhood home, or the phantasm of that home. August in Phoenix turned the home into a cement cage rattled by the endless churn of the dual AC unit. Regina had already mercilessly emptied out the closets, throwing junk that my mom had treasured but my dad probably had forgotten about, into boxes and bags. I cleared off Mom's bookshelves like a spurned lover having a tantrum. Her CD collection went into the egg crates; Dad was about as likely to listen to a Pablo Casals live concert disc as he was to watch *All In with Chris Hayes.*

My mom's stuff had gone almost untouched for two years. I don't think it was out of sentimentality on Dad's part. He was either too depressed, too full of inertia, or too exhausted to do the work, or maybe some degree of all three. My dad had never been a flitting bird of energy anyway; my entire life, I've never known him to watch fewer than seven hours of TV a day, no matter who was around or what was going on. Once the diabetes hit, he spent even more time in the soft chair, watching predictions of liberal-caused doom or shows about barbecue. He was just trying to breathe at night. My mother's old grad-school notebooks were his last concern.

Out they went into the trash. Her old Spanish-English dictionaries and Isabelle Allende novels hit the skids, too. Books of Judaica and Hispanica got dumped along with Diana Gabaldon novels and beach-novel weepers. My dad had one book, a Daniel Silva mystery about an Israeli superspy who is also an art restorer. He'd been nursing the first hundred pages for eighteen months. That one stayed on the shelf along with the photo albums.

I took the books and music to Half Price, which gave me ninety bucks on one visit and another twenty-five on a follow-up, the sum total of what remained of mom's intellectual ambitions on earth.

I spent all the next day on the interstate in Dad's RAV4 in search of a place that could recycle the vast amount of discarded and ancient electronic equipment that had accumulated in my parents' house over the years.

I found a place in deep South Phoenix that refurbished old computers at a junkyard behind a junkyard. Out front, a guy wearing a Statue of Liberty costume was twirling a sign encouraging me to drive on in. Once I got there, another guy looked into my trunk, pulled everything out, and threw it in a pile on the ground.

"What are you going to do with that?" I asked.

"I dunno," he said. "I think we send it to Texas."

When I told Uncle Rick what I'd done with the electronics, he said, "Why didn't you just take them to Best Buy?" They recycled it for free. He's always the smartest guy in the room.

Then came the matter of the remainder of my parents' stuff. There were many more cleanouts to come. My sisters did two. Aunt Estelle did another. It takes a long time to cull a life. But even so, I had bags and boxes full of things I hadn't seen for thirty-five years ready to be put through the recycle bin of life.

I drove to a Goodwill center not far from my parents' house. This wasn't a store, just a windowless storefront in a strip mall, a hot room where dreams die. I knocked on the door. No response. I knocked again. Finally, I heard a sound like chains dragging across concrete. A steel bay door cranked open. There stood an enormous man, looking to be in his late twenties, tongue lolling out of his mouth, sweating.

"WHUUUUUUUUUH?" he said.

"I, um, I was cleaning out my parents' house—my dad just had heart surgery, and I . . ."

He motioned for me to pop the trunk. With a frustrated grunt, he hauled out the first bag, and pitched it inside. I heard glass, or maybe porcelain shatter. I picked up another bag but he waved me off.

"NUUHHHHHHHH," he said.

He bent over and I could see about three-quarters of his ass crack. Then he carelessly tossed another bag of my parents' belongings onto the pile. My entire life's history was a meaningless pile of molecules and I thought, not for the first nor the last time that month, that I could really use some weed right then. But whatever impulse I might have had in that direction, I resisted. And I needed to resist. Because Dad was ready to come home.

• • •

I drove Dad back from the rehab center. He was wearing gray sweatpants, light-brown moccasins, and a pink polo shirt. I'd never seen him wear a collarless shirt unless he was going to the gym.

We parked in the garage and I got his new aluminum walker out of the back of the RAV4. Rebecca had come over to put it together after my initial attempts had flopped. He made his way, slowly, into the house.

Immediately, he clacked into the kitchen and opened the dishwasher, examining the contents.

"Filthy dirty," he said.

Then he went into the backyard. It had been a month since he'd seen it. I watched him through the kitchen window, his expression growing more and more sour. He staggered around, squinting in the August inferno, like his house had just gotten bombed.

Dad came inside.

"My lawn looks like shit," he said.

The grass was two-toned, brown, and crispy. Most of the house had natural desert landscaping, but for decades he had maintained a wood-framed hexagonal patch of grass, not even big enough for a game of croquet, that mostly served as a dog toilet. After my mom died, my cousins and I sat on that grass with our shoes off and talked about how we, too, were going to die very soon.

"You couldn't have taken better care of the pool?" he said. "Why are the pots so crusty?"

Here's where the sobriety kicked in. Maybe in the past, I would have responded with a hearty "FUCK YOU!" and stormed off like a toddler.

"Dad, I am not your pool boy and I am not your maid. I'm here to take you to doctor appointments and make you food if you want me to. Whatever problems you see in the house are not my fault and not my responsibility. Now go sit down and I'll bring you something to eat."

He looked at me confusedly, thinking *this is not the hysterical man-child I raised.* At least that was what I hoped he was thinking.

Later that day, after he napped, we went to Trader Joe's, where I bought him a bunch of food he didn't want to eat, and then I made him that food, and he ate it even though he clearly didn't enjoy it.

"I wish I had my blueberry muffins," he said sadly.

The next morning, the routine began. A nurse came over and took his vitals. An occupational therapist followed, telling him he needed to remove the glass door on his shower and replace it with a plastic shower curtain. The little metal thing on the end of his bed, where he and mom had gathered their bedspread after drawing down for the night, also had to go, because that was a fall hazard.

A physical therapist came over and ran Dad through the exercises. He needed to build some functional strength for a few weeks before starting cardiac rehab, and then the next phase of his life could begin.

And, you know, maybe if Dad had been an ordinary cardiac patient who'd just undergone a common heart surgery, he might have made it to the next phase of his life. But he never made it to cardiac rehab. Every day, I took him to a different doctor. There was the nephrologist who warned Dad that he was in Stage 3 of kidney failure and recommended a little dialysis followed by a lot of dialysis. Then we went to see Dad's GP, who told him he needed to eat better and exercise.

"Your dad isn't as good at coming to see me as he should be," the doctor said.

"How long has it been?" I asked.

"A couple of years," he said.

"I go to enough doctors," Dad said, and then he inquired about a kidney transplant. The doctor informed him that as a seventy-five-year-old diabetic who'd just had quadruple bypass surgery, Dad was not at the top of the list for kidney transplants.

When Dad had still been at the rehab place, I talked to a guy who'd had the same procedure as my dad and who was around the same age. He had a nice tan and nice teeth, and his wife fussed over him while he talked about how he walked three miles a day and played golf and how they had plans to go see Macchu Picchu soon. There are seventy-five-year-old people like this all over Phoenix, living their second adolescence fueled by statins. My dad, a tragic widower, looked sad and shrunken in comparison. It was possible that he wouldn't walk three miles again, total, for the rest of his life. He'd had to give up his *dog* because he couldn't walk him. I felt great compassion for him then, and tremendous fear. Assuming disaster or accident didn't strike first, this was how it would end for all of us.

In the exam room, the nurse had Dad take off his shirt. There was nothing left of him. He looked saggy and wispy, like Gollum. I think a large part of him understood what was happening, but he tried to remain optimistic that the doctors could somehow rescue this collapsing machine. The heart surgeon said he looked okay, all things considered, but there was the possibility they'd have to put in a pacemaker within the next three months.

Another procedure? I thought. How many times were they going to slice this man open?

"What are the odds of that happening?" I asked.

My dad looked at me, annoyed.

"About 50/50," the doctor said. "The heart isn't really working on its own very well."

If the heart couldn't beat on its own, then why do that huge intervention surgery on a guy whose other bodily functions were also collapsing? But I suppose this is why heart surgeons have vacation homes and also other vacation homes. Once you enter the procedure matrix, you rarely escape.

Meanwhile, my dad's hand had ballooned to triple its normal size, as the stent for his forthcoming dialysis was tapped into the wrong artery or some such thing. We went to see a specialist who examined it and determined that, yes, it needed to be reinserted, so there was an appointment for Dad to have another procedure, which would involve more anesthesia and more people sticking more things in his collapsing body.

I'd been managing this situation for ten days now, and boy, did I want to get high. But I didn't. I just kept plugging ahead, every day, controlling the appointments, trying not to get too upset when Dad yelled at me or refused the salad that I'd made him for dinner, or when I heard him say, to a friend on the phone, "He's a pain in my ass but he means well."

My father loved me and said so often, but he didn't *like* me, and never had. The feeling was mutual. The fact that I, of all people, was his primary caregiver, even for a short time, was deeply, sadly ironic. I was an unpaid butler, and he didn't want a butler. We would never have been friends if we hadn't been related. Here we were, doing the end-life dance together. At least I wasn't stoned.

I took him to get re-stented. This took about three hours, check-in to check-out. In the meantime, I went home, emptied out the pill cabinet of any expired or useless prescriptions that he or my mother had left behind, and drove them to a police station, where I dumped them into a metal container in the lobby. Then I went to Pane Bianco in downtown Phoenix, ate three more pieces of pizza than I should have, and also had a glass of wine. I was in recovery from marijuana, not alcohol. I had a glass of wine with dinner about once a month. It was fine, I swear. I half wondered if Dad was going to make it out of the procedure alive.

Then I got to the facility, walked into the back, and there Dad was, sitting up, looking fine.

"Hi," he said.

He was a tough old bear; I'll give him that. The man wanted to live. But he wasn't going to be able to live by himself.

● ● ●

Since it became apparent that Dad wasn't about to have a live-in care person, and that if he lived by himself for more than a few weeks he was going to plotz, my sisters and I had to find somewhere for him to live. Maybe he could have afforded the really nice places, the Ritz-Carltons of senior warehousing, if he sold his house. But they all had three- or four-year waiting lists. He would have needed to be on those lists before my mother died; but when my mother was alive, they didn't need those places.

Becca had picked out a couple of spots in Scottsdale. Dad and I visited the nicer-looking place first. It had a lobby full of gaudy, over-gilded furniture, a little coffee bar in the foyer, and a variety of people, most of whom looked older than my dad, coming in and out of elevators, enthusiastically heading for the cafeteria in anticipation of the 4:30 dinnertime.

Dad and I met with some sort of sales guy, who didn't give too tough of a pitch. They had apartments open. Not the best ones, but decent ones. New ones came open all the time, sometimes in bunches. That was the peril and benefit of a building with a terminal population. They had round-the-clock medical care—if you needed it.

We looked at some apartments. They were okay. They had full kitchens and handicap-accessible tubs. They allowed pets. It wasn't heaven, nor was it hell. I felt like it was somewhat better than purgatory, but not much.

They had good facilities: a movie theater, a gym, a pool, a game room, and a crafts center. There were outings to the outlet mall, the casino, the opera, and the Diamondbacks game. They would take you to the doctor for free within ten miles, or they could call you an Uber, or you could drive yourself.

"I'm hoping I'll be driving soon," Dad said, though that would be hard because his calves had started to fill with fluid and he could barely walk. He seemed to like the place pretty well, though he was most attracted to the frequent snack and juice fridges located all over the common areas. I never thought I'd see the day when my dad could find unlimited juice appealing, but I guess we'd arrived at that point. Really, I don't think he liked it very much at all, but he put on a nice face.

The next facility was like the first one, only worse. During our tour, several residents came up to our guide and complained that the company wasn't making repairs to their condos, or had ignored repeated requests for help. The rep showed us a fully stocked bar next to a movie theater, an abandoned art studio, and several poker tables.

"That's what we do here," she said. "We drink and we gamble."

Well, my dad didn't do *either* of those things, but we did have lunch there. The food was unbelievably lousy, whereas the food at the first place was only moderately lousy. Still, it was food that someone actually cooked. My dad had once prepared great feasts for dozens of people, but now it was a big night in the kitchen if he managed to throw a baked potato in the microwave. For all the diabetic dietary advice the medical community continued to throw at him, all dad really wanted to do was eat blueberry muffins from Costco.

The next day, Dad got up, showered, got dressed, and a friend picked him up and took him to a Rotary meeting. I called Regina and complained for an hour and a half. If I'd been completely selfless about taking care of my dad, I wouldn't have complained to anyone, or written these pages. I would have just done what everyone has done throughout history: sucked it up and done my duty. But regardless, my duty was done. Dad had been in my care for nearly three weeks, and he not only hadn't died on my watch, he'd actually gotten slightly better. I hadn't lost my temper, or my mind, once. And I can only thank sobriety for that. It was a sad time that was about to get a lot sadder, but at least I hadn't made things worse.

That night, Dad and I went out to dinner for the last time. There's a chain restaurant near my house in Austin called Pappadeaux Seafood Kitchen. He loved to eat the oysters at Pappadeaux's.

Phoenix had a Pappadeaux's too, way west and a little north of where Dad lived. We drove there at rush hour. It took quite a long time for oysters that he probably could have gotten at another place much closer to him. But he loved the Pappadeaux's. The place was crowded and we had a bad table, but he didn't care. So I guess I didn't either. He also probably shouldn't have been eating oysters. The man didn't have a gall bladder. But who was I to stop him from his remaining earthly pleasures? Plus, he paid.

I don't remember exactly what Dad and I talked about there in that crowded chain restaurant on the western edge of the Valley. Not much, probably; we didn't have much in common, and we never had. But it was pleasant enough, and he was wearing a nice shirt that covered up the fact that, underneath, he was in an advanced state of decrepitude. We had a pleasant time and didn't argue. There was nothing to argue about anymore.

I was watching episodes of a now-canceled Joel McHale Netflix talk show in my bedroom around midnight when I heard a rustling in the kitchen. Dad was sitting at the table, his head in his hands.

"Are you okay?" I asked.

"My blood sugar dropped to nothing," he said.

"Should I call an ambulance?"

He gasped.

"Get me a glass of apple juice," he said. "Quick."

I did what he asked. He gulped it down. And buried his head in his hands.

"Hit me again," he said.

I did. He gulped down another glass.

"Jesus, Dad," I said.

"I'll be okay," he said. "It's just my blood sugar."

Soon, there'd be no one left to pour him apple juice at midnight when he had a diabetic crash. He still hadn't moved to put his house on the market and hadn't signed a letter of intent with one of the retirement communities. Things were moving too slowly. And there was nothing I could do.

"You take care of yourself," I said.

He was still in bed when I left the next morning.

NO WEDDINGS AND A FUNERAL

In September, Dad signed the papers to move into the decent facility. He didn't seem thrilled about it, but he admitted that he couldn't really take care of himself anymore. His house since 1977, my boyhood home, went on the market. Meanwhile, a former nanny of my sister's moved in with Dad, along with the love of her life, whom she had met at a soap-opera fan convention. The final season of my family's occupation of that house featured Dad living alongside two lesbians in love. He liked the company.

Moving day came. The facility took care of everything. My sisters were on hand to help Dad set everything up. He still had his bedroom set, his TV, and a desk and computer because he was still occasionally working with clients. "I've got everything I need," he said. And he sounded kind of happy.

That didn't last too long. The chef quit in the dining room, and the food, already on the verge of sketchy, went downhill quickly. Uncle Rick came to town to take Dad to his appointment to have a pacemaker put in.

"It's not as fun as it used to be to come here," he texted my sisters and me.

"The fun is over," I texted back.

Dad sold his house, to an Indian doctor. "An Asian Indian, not a woo-woo Indian," he said.

"Are they going to knock it down?" I asked.

"I think they're going to live in it," he said. "But I don't care."

I cared. That house had been the rock of my life. Among other things, on New Year's Eve 1988, I lost my virginity in that house, in what had once been my bedroom but became the place my dad played solitaire.

I'd spent pretty much every Thanksgiving and Passover there. Those were special holidays. At his height, Dad made a masterful turkey and carved it like a surgeon. He also made a matzo ball soup that would have won awards if he'd submitted it for one. He started making it months before, roasting a beef bone as the basis for the broth. By the time Passover arrived, that soup was deeply, extra-dimensionally yellow, a festival of animal essence and schmaltz. But all those traditions were gone. Many of my profound memories, good and bad, took place on that acre plot of land in the desert. And suddenly, it was no more.

I fantasized about going to Phoenix for Thanksgiving and driving by the house, knocking on the door, and asking to see what the new owners had done with the place. The kids would be playing happily, or maybe unhappily, like my sisters and I would have done. If the weather were warm enough, maybe they'd be doing cannonballs into the pool. But I also realized this fantasy verged on insane.

In December, my Aunt Estelle and Uncle Larry went to Phoenix to help Dad clean out the house one final time before an estate sale company came in to sell off whatever remaining possessions he didn't take away to the facility. They went out to breakfast and Dad ordered French toast, smothered in maple syrup and butter. It was pretty much the worst thing a Type 2 diabetic with impending kidney failure could eat.

"Maybe you should order something else?" Estelle said.

"I'll eat what I want," Dad told her.

I called Dad on December 17. He answered the phone, heaving for breath.

"Are you all right?" I said.

"It's just hard to move," he said.

Margot talked to him on December 20. He sounded just as bad. She was worried and called to ask for help. The complex sent some people up to look in on him. When they went into his apartment, they found him at his washer and dryer, doing a load of sheets. He told them to get lost.

My family was getting ready to drive to Nashville to see Regina's mother for Christmas. She and Elijah headed off to do some last-minute errands. As soon as they left, Rebecca called me, sobbing.

"They found Dad," she said. "He died."

She'd called him in the morning, twice, with no response. After a few minutes, she called the facility. They went into his apartment. Dad was on his back on his unmade mattress.

We all like to think that we'll die peacefully in bed, though that's not exactly what happened to him. My dad did die *on* a bed, but he wasn't sleeping. His heart had stopped. I suspect his blood sugar had crashed; he couldn't get to the apple juice one final time.

There hadn't been much joy in Dad's life since mom had died. He'd managed to visit his grandchildren and had one relatively healthy summer, but mostly, it had been a time of loneliness and suffering. At last, his suffering was over.

So instead of driving to Nashville, we headed the opposite direction. Dad still hadn't signed the papers to sell the house, and now my sisters and I owned it jointly. So we could have stayed there for free, one last time.

"You don't want to do that," Rebecca said.

She was right, I didn't. Now the house was a *total* ghost. Rebecca had started working at a hotel and she got rooms for the family. We even sprung for a separate room for Elijah, because no one wants to share a hotel room with a teenager if it can at all be avoided.

My entire family was in Phoenix, and none of us were staying at my parents' house. The foundation of everything I'd ever known had evaporated. And now it was time to say goodbye to Dad.

We buried him at the veterans' cemetery the day after Christmas. Unlike my mom's funeral, which had all the hoopla of an opening night, we held a quiet service under a dusty pergola. But it wasn't an empty affair. Dad had a large family, and lots of friends. He'd lived in Phoenix for a long time and boasted a huge network of business acquaintances. At various times, he'd been president of the B'nai B'rith and of his Rotary chapter. His death wasn't a major news item, but he was loved, and is missed by people all over the world.

As a veteran, my dad got a military funeral. The honor guard played taps and performed an elaborate flag-folding ceremony. A kid who couldn't have been older than nineteen then placed the flag in my lap, which my sisters later agreed was a little bit sexist.

"On behalf of the President of the United States of America, we offer our deepest condolences," he said.

I never thought that at my father's funeral, a teenager would present me with an American flag on behalf of Donald Trump. That is what occurred, though, and I still have that flag.

After the funeral broke up, Margot, Rebecca, and I went to our parents' gravesite, where they allowed us, at a distance, to watch them churn the earth. Mom and Dad would be stacked atop each other in the desert. My mom had always hated Arizona, and my dad only went outside reluctantly, but there they were, for all eternity.

Then it was back to the house, which we still had for another week or so. My sisters had rented chairs and tables and we had a spread from the local deli. People came and went, telling us how much my dad had hated the complex where he ended up dying. They could go suck an egg. I didn't see them lining up to measure his blood sugar and try to serve him three squares a day. Dad would have died no matter where he was living at the end. Maybe he would have been better off just staying at home and expiring in the bedroom where he'd slept most of his life. My sisters and I had tried our best. It didn't matter anymore.

I'd undergone some profound changes in the twenty-one months between the deaths of my parents. At my mom's shiva, I'd been high out of my mind, stumbling in the darkness of grief. By the time my dad died, I wasn't even eating gluten.

As a sober person, I was able to be a little more useful to my sisters. I could run errands for and with them without complaining much. When it came time to do the paperwork— and there was a *lot* of paperwork—I easily handled more than my share. I made a lot of phone calls, closed out accounts, asked the right questions, and generally took on more of the load than they were expecting. This was only possible because I was sober. Not only could I help, but I *wanted* to help. I was happy to be of service, and to prove to them that, for once in my life, I could be useful for something other than pure self-promotion.

"It's like you're a different person," my sister Margot said to me. I don't know if that was true, but maybe I was a slightly less selfish version of the person I'd always been. How many more years would pass before people would be gathering to say goodbye to me? If I was lucky, it'd be thirty or more. But it could easily be fewer. If I'm going to be around for that short of a time, the least I could do is help out the small number of people on earth who actually care.

The shiva ended. As the party cleared out, I lingered, just to have one last look at the place that had framed and defined my entire life. Isn't that what you're supposed to do, wander the rooms and sigh? Margot and Rebecca would return to move all of Dad's furniture, which had just been moved a month before, back into the house. The estate sale, which was supposed to happen when he was alive, now *really* was a clearinghouse. And then they had to throw away still another mound in an endless rotation of household garbage. But I would not set foot in this house again. As informed by a life of watching TV finale episodes, I was B.J. Hunnicutt leaving the rocks on the ground, saying "GOODBYE," Sam Malone turning off the lights in *Cheers* one last time, or maybe little Tommy Westphall gazing into the snow globe as my entire world got shaken upside down like at the end of *St. Elsewhere*. It was the end.

The next day, Regina and I drove Elijah and the dog home, leaving behind whatever remained in Arizona.

● ● ●

Seven months later, we drove to Colorado with the dog, Elijah, and one of his friends. Aunt Estelle had a condo up in the mountains and we met my sister and her family there.

We took the same route that I'd driven back when I'd been a marijuana journalist, through the Panhandle and up into

New Mexico. There, on the other side of the Raton Pass, sat cannabis Cibola: Trinidad, Colorado, which in the succeeding years had completely reshaped its economy and identity around marijuana. A dispensary the size of an airplane hangar sat on the southbound interstate. I saw an old brick building downtown where three of the four storefronts sold marijuana.

Weed was omnipresent. In the spring I'd visited Las Vegas for a trivia championship, and my Uber driver tried to take me to a dispensary. The odor of weed constantly wafted through the vents of my hotel, though admittedly I *was* staying at the Hard Rock. Billboards reminded me, wherever I went, that I could smoke marijuana, I could do it for cheap, and I could do it *right now*.

We drove into Colorado. Pueblo had also added its share of dispensaries, boldly situated along the highway, no longer hiding in the dirt on the access roads. They were *everywhere*. Not so much in conservative Colorado Springs, which only allowed the sale of medical marijuana, but we saw more than our share of neighborhood spots in Denver, where they're almost as common these days as corner bars.

The next day, when we headed up into the mountains, I saw signs like "Last Dispensary for 27 Miles," somewhat odd since twenty-seven miles is really not that far, even on 45-mph mountain roads. Elijah and his friend seemed uncommonly interested in this trend, unseen in Texas.

"People here must smoke a ton of weed," my teenage son said.

"I know I used to," I said.

There were two dispensaries on the main drag of the town where we were staying. All I needed to do was head on down, a couple of twenties in hand, and buy some gummy bears, and then it could all start over again. God knows I was tempted.

I'm always tempted. Every day, I think about marijuana—the fun I had on it, how my body tingled all over when I was high, how much I laughed, and how I could zone out on anything, fascinated, for hours. But I also have to remember the times when my breath smelled like ash, and I yelled at strangers in public, and I ignored my family because all I really wanted to do, ever, was get high and fuck off my responsibilities. And if I'm not mindful, every day, every hour, that could start all over again.

Up there in the mountains, we went for hikes along clear lakes and up to the Continental Divide. We drank coffee and on Clear Creek I "rode the bull"—at least that's what the raft guide called it. I sat at the front and held onto a rope for dear life while freezing mountain water gushed up into my bathing suit. We ate dinner with our family every night, went shopping for coffee and candy, and let the beautiful dog of my dreams cuddle up to us and give us kisses. Mom and Dad were gone. We'd sold my childhood home. But everyone else, my aunts and uncles, my cousins, my nieces and nephews, my dog, my son, and my wife, were still here. Most of the characters in the show of my life remained in the scene, and I was still here too.

Our lives are too short, but also too long. And sometimes the wrong things matter to us. We become obsessed with alcohol, or drugs, or food, or gambling, or sex, or money. No one ever gets a free pass at birth saying they're going to avoid suffering forever. But if you can stay mostly clear of what hurts you most, then at least you have a decent chance at contentment.

We drove all the way to Colorado, stayed for eight days, and drove all the way home, and not once did I get high. Weed was ubiquitous, and it would be for the rest of my life. But it didn't have to be in my house, or my car, or wherever I was walking or laying my head. I was going to be the best husband, father, friend, brother, uncle, nephew, cousin, and person I could be. That might not have been good enough, and compared to other people, I was still probably going to seem like a huge jerk.

Getting sober didn't mean that I'd undergone a huge personality transplant. But for two-plus terrible years, the truck of life had dragged me hard. I bore the scars, at least inside. If I wasn't a different person, then at least I could be a better person, and that had to be enough.

When things go wrong, and they will, I'll try to not make them worse by behaving selfishly, and stupidly. I'm going to live my life in the present moment, with love and empathy. Most of all, I'm going to live it sober.

ACKNOWLEDGMENTS

Many thanks to my agent, Murray Weiss, who saw this project through its many iterations, and who seems to enjoy the challenge of managing my mercurial career. My editor at Central Recovery Press, Bucky Sinister, was enormously helpful and lots of fun. Also thanks to the good people at CRP, in particular Patrick Hughes and Valerie Killeen, for their support, and to Courtney Greenhalgh and Dandelion PR.

My friends Heather Wilhelm, Zack Teibloom, and Rachel Llewellyn read the manuscript at various parts of its development, and I'm grateful for their time and feedback. Also infinite thanks to my family, especially my sisters Margot and Rebecca, for all their love and support. Nothing would be possible without my wife Regina Allen, my son Elijah, and my dog Briar, who can't read but would like this book if she could.

Finally, I dedicate this book to my late parents, Susan and Bernard Pollack. Miss you, mom and dad. But we're all doing OK.